A Literary Picnic: Extended Edition

9 MENUS OF OUTDOOR-FRIENDLY RECIPES INSPIRED BY CLASSIC LITERATURE

BY
ALISON WALSH

For Francis, Fabian, and Fatima

Copyright © 2024 by Alison Walsh

All rights reserved. No part of this book may be reproduced in any manner without the express written consent of the author, except in the case of brief excerpts in critical reviews or articles. All inquiries should be addressed to alisonswonderlandrecipes@gmail.com.

10 9 8 7 6 5 4 3 2 1

Cover design by Alison Walsh
Cover and interior illustrations from Canva
Photographs by Alison Walsh

Print ISBN: 979-8-9908406-0-7
Ebook ISBN: 979-8-9908406-1-4

Letter From the Author

Dear Reader,

Welcome to *A Literary Picnic!* This book marks my first foray into self-publishing. It's been quite the rollercoaster! From learning to format a manuscript to navigating the distribution process, I've become a woman of many hats. I kinda love it! For years, I wanted to create a book of literary picnic recipes. It's been so freeing to come up with a design vision for my book and develop the skills to bring it to life myself.

As with all my cookbooks, *A Literary Picnic* is for readers of all culinary skill levels. Whether you're a kitchen novice or a seasoned home cook, you'll find recipes here that were made with you in mind. For beginners, I highly recommend the Chamomile Muffins (p. 87) and Honey Almond Granola Bars (p. 104). For those who want to flex their skills, the Vanilla Bean Marshmallow Bunnies (p. 89) and Chocolate Raspberry Cream Puffs (p. 97) are great options. Yet even the "difficult" recipes are written to feel approachable because I firmly believe that high culinary skill should not be a prerequisite for enjoying food from your favorite literature.

Within these pages, you'll find nine menus with five recipes each: appetizer, entrée, side dish, dessert, and beverage. Each one is designed with outdoor dining in mind—easy to prep ahead, transport, and enjoy on the go. And they're almost all finger foods! Most are servable at room temperature and can sit outdoors for a couple hours. Still, for best results it's always a good idea to store food in sealed containers in a shady spot or cooler until ready to serve.

So grab a picnic basket, your favorite book, and a snack for the road—the summer sun is calling!

Love,
Alison

Contents

Dedication 2

Letter From the Author 3

Alice in Wonderland

The Queen of Hearts Tarts 10

Card Suit Tea Sandwiches 12

Mushroom Scones 14

"We're All Mad Here" Dessert 17

Drink Me Potion 21

Anne of Green Gables

Delightful Applesauce 25

Curried Carrot & Chicken Sandwiches . . . 27

French Carrot Salad 28

Marilla's Plum Puffs 29

Raspberry Cordial Italian Soda 31

Fairy Tales

Fairy Bread 34

Rapunzel's Braided Pastries 36

Red Riding Hood's Red Fruit Salad 38

Enchanted Swan Cookies 39

Poison Apple Punch 43

Jane Austen

Mini Bath Buns 46

Mini "Pigeon" Pies 48

Strawberry Fool in a Jar 51

Regency Bride Cake 53

Citrus Mead Punch 54

Little Women

Orchard House Salad 59

Jo's Corned Beef & Potato Roll Sandwiches . . 60

Pickled Limes with Dried Fruit 62

Blanc Mange with Strawberries 65

Plumfield Iced Tea 67

Peter Pan

Peter Hat Chips & Dip 71

Ham and Cheese Pirate Ships 73

Neverland Tropical Fruit Salad 74

Peter's Cake 75

Fairy Dust Punch 79

Peter Rabbit

Blackberry Almond Croissant Bake 83

Carrot Apple Hand Pies 85

Chamomile Muffins 87

Vanilla Bean Marshmallow Bunnies 89

Strawberry Lavender Chamomile Iced Tea 91

The Secret Garden

Herbed Key Crackers 94

Fruit & Flower Chicken Salad Croissants 95

Garden Gate Salad 96

Chocolate Raspberry Cream Puffs 97

Sparkling Rose Lemonade 101

Winnie-the-Pooh

Honey Almond Granola Bars 104

Rabbit's Garden Wraps 105

Tigger Stripe Fruit Leather 109

Honey Clementine Cupcakes 110

Eeyore's "Feeling Blue" Iced Lattes 113

Helpful Odds & Ends

Printable Menus 115

Recipe Testing Log 124

Recipe Card 125

Cooking Tips 126

Conversion Chart 127

About the Author 128

Reference List 129

Index 130

Alice in Wonderland

Here you will find everything you need to host the perfect Mad Tea Party: mini tarts, tea sandwiches, scones, and color-changing Drink Me Potion. To top it all off, what looks like a teacup, spoon, and saucer is really dessert: tea jelly and cookies in disguise!

The Queen of Hearts Tarts	10
Card Suit Tea Sandwiches	12
Mushroom Scones	14
"We're All Mad Here" Dessert	17
Drink Me Potion	21

The Queen of Hearts Tarts

MAKES 10 TARTS

"In the very middle of the court was a table, with a large dish of tarts upon it: they looked so good, that it made Alice quite hungry to look at them—'I wish they'd get the trial done,' she thought, 'and hand round the refreshments!'"

Many recipes for the Queen of Hearts Tarts are sweet, but these take a savory direction: almond pie crust, Camembert filling, and a raspberry amaretto jam topping.

INGREDIENTS

For the Crust
- ½ cup sliced almonds
- 1¼ cups flour
- 1 tsp salt
- ½ cup cold unsalted butter, cut into cubes
- 4-6 Tbsp very cold water
- 2½" heart cookie cutter

For the Filling
- ½ cup raspberry jam
- 2 Tbsp amaretto
- 4 oz Camembert cheese, diced
- 20 sliced almonds (reserved from crust)

STEP 1. Toast the almonds on a baking sheet at 325°F for 5 minutes. Allow to cool on the pan. Reserve 20 whole slices for garnish. Grind the rest to use for the crust (it should come out to about ¼ cup plus 1 Tbsp). Combine all the crust ingredients except the water in a food processor and process on low for 30-60 seconds or until the butter cubes are pea-sized with slightly larger clumps of butter scattered throughout. Transfer to a large bowl. Work in the water with a fork 1-2 Tbsp at a time until the mix is damp and holds together when pressed but isn't soggy. Shape into a disk and wrap tightly in plastic wrap. Refrigerate for 1 hour.

STEP 2. While the dough chills, preheat the oven to 375°F. In a small saucepan, heat the jam and amaretto over medium-high heat until simmering. Reduce heat to medium-low and cook for 8 minutes, stirring continuously. Transfer to a bowl and allow to cool to room temperature uncovered, stirring every 10 minutes or so to prevent a skin from forming.

STEP 3. On a floured surface, roll out the dough into a 13" x 13" circle (just shy of ¼" thick) and cut out 10 hearts with a cookie cutter. Lay the hearts on a baking sheet lined with parchment paper. Place in the fridge. Cut 10 ¾" x 8" strips from the dough, gathering and rerolling the extra dough if necessary. Remove baking sheet from fridge. Brush the edge of a heart with water and gently press a strip of dough around the edge to make a wall, making sure to press together the ends securely. Pinch the top of the heart where the two curves meet so that it makes a point to help the tart keep a defined shape while baking. See photo at left for reference. Prick the center of the heart 3 times with a fork. Repeat with all hearts.

Continues on next page.

Step 4. Bake for 13 minutes. The walls of the tarts should not crack, but if they do, it's ok. They should still be able to hold the filling without leaks.

STEP 5. Fill each heart with a layer of Camembert and heat for 5 minutes. Spread ½ Tbsp of the cooled jam over the top of the Camembert. Add 2 almond slices in the shape of a heart on top of each tart. Bake for 10 more minutes or until the edges are golden brown.

STEP 6. Allow to cool for 5 minutes on the pan. Transfer to a wire rack to cool completely. Refrigerate. If you would like to warm them before transporting to a picnic, place them on a baking sheet in a 350°F oven for 10 minutes. Pack in a single layer in a covered, heat-safe baking dish.

Serve to the Queen of Hearts!

 # Card Suit Tea Sandwiches

MAKES 12 SANDWICHES

"First came ten soldiers carrying clubs . . . oblong and flat, with their hands and feet at the corners: next the ten courtiers; these were ornamented all over with diamonds . . . After these came the royal children . . . they were all ornamented with hearts."

Making your own jams and nut butters is super easy and a great way to avoid added preservatives and corn syrup. This recipe includes instructions for almond butter, and you can check out my Fairy Bread recipe (p. 34) to find out how to make your own blackberry jam.

INGREDIENTS

- **2 cups sliced almonds**
- **pinch of salt**
- **3 Tbsp almond butter (1.5 oz)**
- **12 slices sandwich bread (you will want wide slices of bread to accommodate the size of the cookie cutters. I used Pepperidge Farm Farmhouse Hearty White bread)**
- **2" heart, diamond, spade, and club cookie cutters**
- **2 Tbsp (2 oz) seedless blackberry jam**
- **2 Tbsp (1 oz) Swiss almond cold pack spreadable cheese (such as Merkt or Shullsburg)**
- **6 slices prosciutto**

STEP 1. Preheat oven to 325°F. Spread out the almonds on a baking sheet and toast for 7-9 minutes until lightly browned and fragrant, stirring halfway through. Allow to rest on the pan for 5 minutes. With the almonds still warm, transfer to a food processor with the salt and process for 60 second intervals for 10 minutes. Since this is a long time to run a processor, stop every 1-2 minutes to let the motor rest for half a minute and scrape down the bowl if needed. First the mixture will be grainy, then clump into a ball, then gradually get smooth and pourable (it will firm up when refrigerated). Transfer finished almond butter to a sealable container and refrigerate until ready to use.

STEP 2. Trim the crust from the bread and cut each piece into 2 rectangles (approximately 2½" x 3" in size). You will have 24 total rectangles.

STEP 3. To make the spade/club sandwiches, spread almond butter onto 6 rectangles, making sure to go right up to the edges. You will need 3 Tbsp (1.5 oz) almond butter. Spread blackberry jam on top. Set aside. Using the cookie cutters, cut a spade from the center of 3 new rectangles and a club from another 3. Place these rectangles on top of the ones covered with jam.

Continues on next page.

Note: Don't waste those bread trimmings—make croutons! Cut crusts into cubes and add to a large bowl. Drizzle 2-4 Tbsp olive oil down the sides of bowl and stir until well-coated. Add salt and garlic powder to taste and stir. Bake at 325°F for 15-20 minutes on an ungreased baking sheet and allow to cool on a wire rack.

STEP 4. To make the heart/diamond sandwiches, spread Swiss almond cheese onto 6 rectangles, making sure to go right up to the edges. Fold each slice of prosciutto in half widthwise and trim to fit. Place the prosciutto on top of the cheese-covered rectangles. Cut a heart from the center of 3 new rectangles and a diamond from another 3. Place these rectangles on top of the ones covered with prosciutto.

STEP 5. Tightly cover with plastic wrap and refrigerate until ready to serve. You can also drape a lightly damp paper towel over the sandwiches to keep them from drying out.

Serve to the playing card soldiers!

Mushroom Scones

MAKES 5 SCONES

"After a while she remembered that she still held the pieces of mushroom in her hands, and she set to work very carefully nibbling first at one and then the other."

The trick to tall, fluffy, flaky scones? Cold butter, plenty of raising agent, and resisting the temptation to roll them too flat! You want your dough about ¾" thick. You'll thank me later!

INGREDIENTS

- **2 cups flour**
- **2½ tsp baking powder**
- **¾ tsp baking soda**
- **½ tsp salt**
- **6 Tbsp cold butter, cut into tablespoons**
- **¼ cup finely chopped mushrooms**
- **2 Tbsp bacon bits**
- **1 red mini sweet pepper, minced**
- **1 tsp fresh thyme**
- **1 egg, lightly beaten**
- **¾ cup half and half, divided**
- **¼ tsp kosher salt, for sprinkling**

STEP 1. Preheat oven to 425°F. Line a baking sheet with parchment paper and set aside.

STEP 2. In a large bowl, whisk together the flour, baking powder, baking soda, and salt. With a fork or pastry blender, cut in the butter until the mix has a crumb-like texture with bits of pea-sized butter throughout.

STEP 3. Add the mushrooms, bacon, sweet pepper, and thyme. Stir until combined. Make a well in the center.

STEP 4. Add the beaten egg and ½ cup half and half to the well. Stir with a fork until mixture is just combined. The dough should be just damp enough to come together (don't overwork it, since that can make the scones tough). If you don't have enough moisture to bring all the dry material together, add another 2-3 tablespoons half and half.

STEP 5. Shape the dough into a ball with your hands, making sure to press any stray bits from the bottom of the bowl into the ball. Place it on a floured cutting board. Roll it out into an 7" x 9" rectangle and cut into 4 3-inch circles, re-flouring as needed. Gather the scraps into a ball and re-roll until about ¾" thick. Cut out 1 more circle. Transfer all circles to the baking sheet.

STEP 6. Brush the top of the circles with remaining half and half (you don't have to use it all). Lightly sprinkle with kosher salt.

Continues on next page.

STEP 7. Bake for about 17 minutes until risen and the tops are golden brown.

STEP 8. Allow to cool on the pan for 5 minutes. Transfer to a wire rack to cool completely. Store at room temperature in a sealed container.

Serve during your next visit to Wonderland!

We're All Mad Here
A Dessert That Isn't As It Seems

MAKES 8 TEACUPS AND SAUCERS, 12 SPOONS AND TEABAGS

"'But I don't want to go among mad people,' Alice remarked. 'Oh, you can't help that,' said the Cat: 'We're all mad here. I'm mad. You're mad.' 'How do you know I'm mad?' said Alice. 'You must be,' said the Cat, 'or you wouldn't have come here.'"

This tea setting is dessert in disguise: tea jelly in a teacup, a pizzelle saucer, and spoons and teabags made from tea-flavored sugar cookies.

INGREDIENTS

For the Spoons, Teabags, and Saucers
- 2 Tbsp milk
- 1 tsp loose leaf blackberry tea, divided
- 1 cup flour
- ¼ tsp baking powder
- ⅛ tsp salt
- 5 Tbsp butter, softened
- ¼ cup plus 2 Tbsp sugar
- ½ egg
- 1 tsp vanilla
- 2" teabag cookie cutter
- 4 oz 60% dark chocolate
- Kitchen twine
- Silicone candy mold for 8 5¼" x 1" spoons
- 3 tsp vodka
- 1 tsp silver luster dust
- 8 vanilla pizzelle cookies
- Extra vodka and gold luster dust, optional

For the Tea Jelly
- 2 cups cold water
- 8 0.25-oz packets unflavored gelatin powder
- 8 bags loose leaf black tea (I used cream flavored tea)
- 4 cups boiling water
- ¼ cup plus 2 Tbsp honey

STEP 1. For the spoons and teabags, warm the milk in the microwave just until steaming. Stir in ½ tsp tea leaves and steep for 4 minutes. Discard used tea leaves and set milk in the refrigerator to cool. In a medium bowl, stir together the flour, remaining tea leaves, baking powder, and salt. Set aside.

STEP 2. In the bowl of a stand mixer fitted with a paddle attachment, beat the butter and sugar on medium-high speed until fluffy, stopping to scrape the sides of the bowl if necessary. Beat in the egg, 1 Tbsp cooled milk*, and vanilla.

STEP 3. On low speed, gradually beat in the flour mix. Gradually adjust the speed to medium-high, beating until just combined. Stop to scrape the sides of the bowl if needed.

STEP 4. Divide and flatten the dough into 2 4" disks. Wrap tightly with plastic wrap and refrigerate for 1 hour or until firm but not hard.

STEP 5. Preheat oven to 325°F. On a floured surface, roll out the first disk to ⅛" thickness and cut out 8 teabags. Gather and reroll remaining scraps. Cut out 4 more teabags. Wrap remaining scraps in plastic wrap and refrigerate, saving them to use for the spoon cookies if needed. Place the teabags evenly apart on an ungreased baking sheet and bake for 8 minutes. Transfer to a wire rack to cool. When the teabags are cool, melt the chocolate and dip the bottom half of each teabag. Rotate the cookie over the chocolate to allow excess to drip off. Place on a sheet of wax paper to set. Cut short lengths of kitchen twine, thread them through the holes in the teabags, and tie them off.

Continues on next page.

*The reason we steep the tea in a little extra milk is because some volume will be lost to steam or soaked into the tea leaves. You can save any leftover steeped milk for the next time you decide to make a cup of tea. It will make it extra flavorful!

NOTE: Feel free to choose any flavor of black tea you want for both the jelly and the cookie dough. I used blackberry for the cookies, but most fruit flavors work equally well.

STEP 6. Remove second disk from the refrigerator and press dough firmly into the 8-spoon mold until it is flush with the top of the wells in the mold, making sure it fills all the gaps on the bottom. A good way to do this is to press down on the edges of the spoon shape so the sides bow out slightly. Place the mold on a baking sheet and bake for 20-23 minutes. Allow to cool in the mold for 10 minutes, then transfer to a wire rack to cool completely. Use remaining dough to make 4 more spoons (if you run out of cookie dough, you can use the scraps you saved from the teabags). Bake and cool as before.

STEP 7. In a small bowl, thoroughly stir together the vodka and silver luster dust, and brush it on the spoon cookies with a food decorating brush. Place the cookies on a sheet of wax paper to dry. If desired, you can use extra vodka/luster dust to decorate the pizzelles. If doing so, use 1 tsp luster dust for every 3 tsp vodka.

STEP 8. When the teabags, spoons, and pizzelle saucers are completely set/dried, store each kind separately in flat layers in tightly sealed containers, with wax paper between each layer. I recommend dipping the cookies in chocolate no more than 3 days before serving, since the chocolate will start to bloom after approximately 5 days.

STEP 9. For the tea jelly, pour the cold water into a medium bowl. Gradually whisk the gelatin into the bowl with a fork. Set aside for 5 minutes.

STEP 10. While the gelatin blooms, steep tea in the boiling water for 4 minutes. Discard tea leaves. Whisk in honey. Gradually whisk the tea into the bowl of gelatin until smooth. Pour into 8 teacups and refrigerate for 1 hour or until set. Store in the fridge with plastic wrap lightly pressed against the top of the tea jelly for up to 3 weeks before serving.

Serve at a Mad Tea Party!

Drink Me Potion

MAKES APPROXIMATELY 7 CUPS

"This time she found a little bottle on it . . . and round the neck of the bottle was a paper label, with the words 'DRINK ME' beautifully printed on it in large letters."

This magic potion starts off a deep blue then changes to pinkish purple when you add the ginger ale and lemon juice!

INGREDIENTS

- 2 Tbsp dried whole butterfly pea flower blossoms
- ¾ cup honey
- 3 cups ginger ale
- ¾ cup lemon juice

STEP 1. Heat 3 cups water in a tea kettle just until steaming (don't let it whistle). Transfer hot water to a pitcher with the butterfly pea flower. Steep for 5 minutes. The tea will brew blue. Discard pea flower. Whisk in honey until dissolved. Refrigerate until cold. In a separate pitcher, stir together the ginger ale and lemon juice. When ready to serve, fill glasses half full with butterfly pea flower tea. Then fill remaining half with ginger ale mix.

Serve to guests at your next unbirthday party . . . and watch the drink turn from blue to pinkish purple!

Anne of Green Gables

In *Anne of Green Gables*, Anne plans a "golden picnic" with her friends to celebrate spring. Now, you can have a golden picnic of your own! Feast on elegant French carrot salad, applesauce inspired by the White Way of Delight, and Italian soda made with homemade raspberry cordial. And don't forget Marilla's famous plum puffs!

Delightful Applesauce 25

Curried Carrot & Chicken Sandwiches ... 27

French Carrot Salad 28

Marilla's Plum Puffs 29

Raspberry Cordial Italian Soda 31

Delightful Applesauce

MAKES 6 CUPS

"Overhead was one long canopy of snowy, fragrant bloom. Below the boughs the air was full of a purple twilight and far ahead a glimpse of painted sunset sky shone like a great rose window at the end of a cathedral aisle . . . 'Oh, Mr. Cuthbert,' she whispered, 'that place we came through—that white place . . . They should call it—let me see—the White Way of Delight.'" — Anne of Green Gables

Apples are mentioned frequently in *Anne of Green Gables* as snacks, and the blossoms are often used as decoration. This recipe is inspired by my favorite mention of apples in the book, Anne's first trip through the Avenue, a road lined with blossoming apple trees, which she affectionately dubs the White Way of Delight.

INGREDIENTS

- 3 lb Gala apples
- 3 lb Pink Lady apples
- 2 Tbsp honey
- 1 cup apple juice
- Zest of 1 orange (about 2 tsp)
- 2 Tbsp fresh orange juice
- 3 cinnamon sticks
- 1 oz fresh ginger, peeled and cut in half
- ¼ tsp salt

STEP 1. Peel the apples. Cut each one into 4 pieces and cut away the core. Combine all ingredients in a large pot over medium heat. Stir to combine.

STEP 2. Cover the pot and cook for 25 minutes, stirring occasionally. Turn off heat and discard cinnamon sticks and ginger. The ginger will be the same color as the apples but is very dense and won't mash (it's sometimes easier to find the ginger once you start mashing).

STEP 3. Mash the apples with a potato masher or heavy glass to desired consistency. Additionally, the apples can be transferred to a blender for an ultra smooth texture.

STEP 4. Transfer to an airtight container and refrigerate until ready to use. Applesauce can also be frozen, then thawed in the refrigerator for two days before serving.

Serve to Anne on her first day at Green Gables!

Curried Carrot & Chicken Sandwiches

MAKES 6-9 SANDWICHES

"Mrs. Pendexter said little; she merely smiled with her lovely eyes and lips, and ate chicken and fruit cake and preserves with such exquisite grace that she conveyed the impression of dining on ambrosia and honeydew." — Anne of Avonlea

Curried chicken may seem like an unusual choice for a Green Gables menu, but it appears in many cookbooks of the time. Curry powder was (and still is) a popular Canadian ingredient.

INGREDIENTS

For the Buttermilk Biscuits
- 2½ cups flour
- 3 tsp baking powder
- ¼ tsp baking soda
- ½ tsp salt
- ½ cup butter, FROZEN
- 1¼ cup buttermilk, cold
- 1 egg
- 1 Tbsp milk
- 2½" circle cookie cutter

For the Filling
- 4 cups cubed cooked chicken
- 1 cup shredded carrot
- 1 cup hummus (see recipe on p. 105)
- 2 tsp lemon juice
- 1 tsp each of cumin, garlic powder, and ginger
- ¾ tsp tumeric and salt
- ½ tsp onion powder
- 4 chopped green onions, green portion only

STEP 1. Preheat oven to 400°F. For the buttermilk biscuits, start by stirring together the flour, baking powder, baking soda, and salt in a large bowl.

STEP 2. Grate the frozen butter into the flour mix using the coarse side of a cheese grater. Stir to combine. Quickly stir in the buttermilk until just combined. On a floured surface, roll out the dough to ½" thickness.

STEP 3. Fold dough in half and reroll to ½" thickness. Fold and roll to the same thickness once more. Finish by folding and rolling the dough into a 1" thick rectangle. Use the cookie cutter to cut out 6 circles, cutting straight down without twisting. If desired, gather and reroll the scraps and cut 2-3 more circles. Evenly space circles on a baking sheet. Whisk the egg and milk together in a small bowl and brush on top of the circles. Bake for 15-17 minutes until golden on top. Allow to cool on a wire rack.

STEP 4. For the filling, stir everything together until well combined. Cut biscuits in half widthwise and fill with ⅓ cup chicken mix.

STEP 5. If making ahead, the curried chicken and biscuits can be frozen in separate sealed containers (place the biscuits in a single layer in their container). Thaw in a refrigerator for 24 hours before serving.

Serve to Anne and her friends on a glorious summer day in Avonlea!

French Carrot Salad

MAKES 4 SMALL SALADS

"Gilbert reached across the aisle, picked up the end of Anne's long red braid, held it out at arm's length, and said in a piercing whisper: 'Carrots! Carrots!' Then Anne looked at him with a vengeance! She did more than look. She sprang to her feet. . . And then—thwack! Anne had brought her slate down on Gilbert's head and cracked it—slate not head—clear across." — Anne of Green Gables

Called "carottes râpées" in it's native French, this carrot salad is simple yet elegant. After a taste of this, even Anne Shirley might learn to love carrots!

INGREDIENTS

- **6 medium carrots, peeled**
- **1 Tbsp snipped fresh parsley**
- **1 Tbsp olive oil**
- **1 tsp lemon zest**
- **1 tsp fresh lemon juice**
- **½ tsp fresh grated ginger**
- **¼ tsp salt**
- **⅛ tsp cumin**
- **⅛ tsp fresh black pepper**

STEP 1. Use a vegetable peeler to cut the carrots into ribbons. To do this, start at the base of the carrot, slide the peeler to the bottom, rotate the carrot 90°, and repeat. Keep doing this until it is too difficult to peel. Set aside carrot cores (these can be frozen and used to make soup stock). Place the carrot ribbons in a medium bowl and set aside.

STEP 2. In a small bowl, whisk together remaining ingredients with a fork. Add to the bowl of carrots and toss to combine.

Serve to Gilbert Blythe after her apologizes for calling Anne "carrots"!

Marilla's Plum Puffs

MAKES 8 PLUM PUFFS

"The cheerful supper table, with the twins' bright faces, and Marilla's matchless plum puffs . . . of which Davy ate four . . . did 'hearten her up' considerably after all." — Anne of Avonlea

These plum puffs are truly worth raving about, and they're so easy! Just add some sliced plums to some puff pastry squares, top with a bit of brown sugar and ginger, and bake! They're sweet, tart, and truly delightful.

INGREDIENTS

- 2 plums
- 1 sheet puff pastry dough, thawed
- 1 egg
- 1 Tbsp brown sugar, packed
- ¼ tsp ground ginger
- ¼ tsp salt
- 1 tsp turbinado sugar
- 1 tsp chopped mint, optional

STEP 1. Preheat oven to 400°F. Line 2 baking sheets with parchment paper and set aside. Cut each plum in half and remove the pits. Cut each half into 10 slices approximately ¼" thick. Set aside.

STEP 2. Roll the puff pastry sheet into a 10" x 12" rectangle. Cut into 8 5" x 3" rectangles. Place rectangles evenly apart on the prepared baking sheets. Whisk egg with 1 tablespoon water. Brush on top of puff pastry.

STEP 3. Partially overlap 5 plum slices across the top of each puff pastry rectangle. Sprinkle with brown sugar, ginger, and salt. Sprinkle turbinado sugar around the exposed edges of the puff pastry. Bake for 8 minutes. Flip and rotate the pans, then bake 8 minutes more. Remove to a wire rack to cool. If desired, top with chopped mint for garnish.

STEP 4. If making ahead, freeze in a single layer in an airtight container and thaw in a refrigerator for 24 hours before serving. They will soften a bit during thawing. Re-warm in a 350°F oven for 8 minutes.

Serve to Davy and Dora to welcome them to Green Gables!

Raspberry Cordial Italian Soda

MAKES 8 SERVINGS

"When Anne came back from the kitchen Diana was drinking her second glassful of cordial; and, being entreated thereto by Anne, she offered no particular objection to the drinking of a third. The tumblerfuls were generous ones and the raspberry cordial was certainly very nice." — Anne of Green Gables

No *Anne of Green Gables* menu is complete without raspberry cordial! This recipe takes it one step further and uses homemade raspberry cordial to make Italian soda. If you're serving this outside on a hot day and are concerned that the recipe includes dairy, feel free to leave out the half and half. This soda is still delicious without it!

INGREDIENTS

- **4 cups frozen raspberries**
- **½ cup honey**
- **2 cups water**
- **1 cup crushed iced**
- **2 cups club soda**
- **1 cup half and half**
- **Fresh raspberries, optional**

STEP 1. To make the raspberry cordial, combine the frozen raspberries, honey, and water in a medium saucepan. Place over medium-high heat, stirring until the raspberries have thawed. Bring mixture to a boil. Reduce heat to medium-low and simmer for 5 minutes.

STEP 2. Place a wire mesh strainer over a medium bowl and press the mixture through the strainer with a spatula. Press firmly several times to get all the juice out, making sure to scrape the bottom of the strainer. Transfer to a sealable container. Cover and refrigerate 1-2 hours until cold.

STEP 3. When ready to serve, add 2 tablespoons crushed ice to a small cocktail glass. Pour in 6 tablespoons raspberry cordial. Add ¼ cup club soda. Top with 2 tablespoons half and half. If desired, garnish with a fresh raspberry.

STEP 4. Repeat Step 2 with remaining ingredients and glasses.

Serve to Diana Barry . . . but don't get it mixed up with the currant wine!

Fairy Tales

For this menu, I imagined a children's brithday party. The food combos are perfect for young palates, but they would also make for an enchanting baby shower!

Fairy Bread 34

Rapunzel's Braided Pastries 36

Red Riding Hood's Red Fruit Salad . . 38

Enchanted Swan Cookies 39

Poison Apple Punch 43

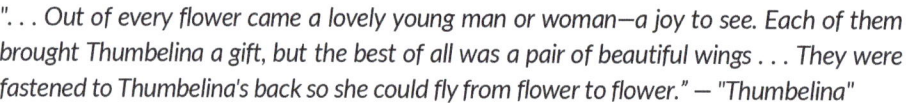

Fairy Bread

MAKES 10 SLICES OF FAIRY BREAD

". . . Out of every flower came a lovely young man or woman—a joy to see. Each of them brought Thumbelina a gift, but the best of all was a pair of beautiful wings . . . They were fastened to Thumbelina's back so she could fly from flower to flower." — "Thumbelina"

Fairy bread is a beloved snack of children in Australia. Traditionally prepared as buttered sandwich bread topped with sprinkles, this version is made with toasted brioche and mascarpone blended with three flavors of homemade jam.

INGREDIENTS

- 8 oz frozen peaches, about 2 cups
- 1¼ cups honey, divided
- ¼ cup plus 2 tsp lemon juice, divided
- 3 pinches of salt, divided
- 1 lb frozen blackberries, about 4 cups
- 1 lb frozen raspberries, about 4 cups
- 7.5 oz mascarpone, divided
- Yellow, pink, and purple gel food coloring (optional)*
- 1 loaf vanilla brioche
- Rainbow sprinkles for garnish

*If you choose to leave out the coloring, the fairy bread will still be colorful, just less vibrant. For color comparison, the photo on p. 32 shows this recipe without food coloring, and p. 35 shows it with food coloring.

STEP 1. For the peach jam, allow peaches to thaw. Blend in a blender until smooth. Transfer to a small saucepan with ¼ cup honey, 2 tsp lemon juice, and a pinch of salt. Stir to combine. Place over medium-high heat and bring to a boil. Reduce heat to medium-low and simmer for 10 minutes, stirring regularly. Transfer to a sealable jar and allow to cool completely on the counter. Seal and refrigerate until ready to use.

STEP 2. For the blackberry and raspberry jams, allow berries to thaw. Transfer each type of berry to a medium saucepan with ½ cup honey, 2 Tbsp lemon juice and a pinch of salt. Stir to combine (for the blackberries, mash thoroughly with a potato masher). Place over medium-high heat and bring to a boil. Reduce heat to medium-low and simmer for 25 minutes, stirring regularly. Pass thoroughly through a wire mesh strainer and transfer to a sealable jar (be sure to scrape the bottom of the strainer as well). Allow to cool completely on the counter before sealing and refrigerating.

STEP 3. In a small bowl, stir together 2.5 oz mascarpone, 3 Tbsp peach jam, and 1 drop yellow gel food coloring. Repeat in separate bowls with the blackberry jam/purple coloring and raspberry jam/pink coloring. Transfer yellow mix to a piping bag fitted with a small star tip, pink mix to a bag with a medium star tip, and purple mix to a bag with a large star tip. Set aside.

Continues on next page.

Note: Why use frozen fruit? It's packed at peak season, which ensures the best quality, and it's usually cheaper than fresh fruit.

STEP 4. Slice 10 thick slices of brioche and toast them. Pipe 9 yellow stars on the right side of each slice, 6 pink stars in the middle, and 3 purple stars on the left.

STEP 5. These can be made the night before serving. Store in the fridge loosely covered. Add sprinkles before serving.

Serve to the fae folk to encourage them to favor you!

Rapunzel's Braided Pastries

MAKES 8 PASTRIES

"Rapunzel had beautiful long hair that shone like gold. When she heard the voice of the witch she would undo the fastening of the upper window, unbind the plaits of her hair, and let it down twenty ells below, and the witch would climb up by it." — "Rapunzel"

These pastries are painted with an edible egg wash "R" for Rapunzel, but you can also use the first letter of the guest of honor at your party.

INGREDIENTS

- ¾ lb ground pork
- ¼ cup panko crumbs
- ¼ cup diced onion
- 1 clove garlic, minced
- 1 tsp snipped fresh thyme
- ½ tsp salt
- ⅛ tsp pepper
- 2½ eggs
- 4 sheets frozen puff pastry, thawed
- 1½" flower cookie cutter
- Pink, blue, and purple gel food coloring

STEP 1. Preheat oven to 375°F. Line two baking sheets with parchment paper and set aside. In a large bowl, mix together the pork, panko crumbs, onion, garlic, thyme, salt, pepper, and ½ an egg until fully combined. Do not overmix. Set aside.

STEP 2. Roll out 1 puff pastry sheet to about 13" x 13" (keep the other sheets in the refrigerator). Trim to make a 12" x 12" square. Cut into 9 4-inch squares. Transfer 4 squares to a prepared baking sheet. Scoop 2 Tbsp filling into the center of each square. Brush the edges with water and place 4 more squares on top, pressing the edges to adhere (you will have 1 square left). Cut remaining square into 8 flowers using a 1½" cookie cutter and set aside. If needed, you can gather and reroll the scraps to cut the last 2 flowers.

STEP 3. Repeat Step 2 to make 4 more pastries and 8 more flowers. Lay all the flowers on the baking sheets between the pastries and cover the baking sheets with damp (but not wet) paper towels. This will keep your pastries from drying out while you work on the braids.

STEP 4. Roll 1 puff pastry sheet to about 13" x 13". Trim to make a 12" x 12" square. Cut into 12 strips and braid into 4 braids. Place completed braids on a large plate covered with a damp paper towel. When finished, cut each braid into 4 3-inch lengths, pinching the ends firmly to prevent unraveling.

STEP 5. Repeat Step 4 with the last sheet of puff pastry.

Continues on next page.

*If you don't have a food brush, you can fold down the bristles of a pastry brush (except for one outside edge) and use the tip of that edge as you would a brush.

STEP 6. Whisk remaining 2 eggs in a small bowl. Brush the pastry squares with egg wash and gently press braids into place to adhere. Brush the braids with egg wash. Divide remaining egg wash evenly between 3 small bowls. Add 1 drop pink coloring to the first bowl, 1 drop blue to the second, and 2 drops purple to the third. Whisk to distribute coloring.

STEP 7. Brush pink egg wash on 8 flowers and blue on the other 8. Firmly press a pink flower on the top right corner of each pastry and a blue flower on the bottom left. Use a food brush to paint a stylized purple "R" onto each pastry.*

STEP 8. Bake for 26-28 minutes or until golden brown, flipping and rotating the pans halfway through. Allow to cool on the pan for 5 minutes. Transfer to a wire rack to cool completely. If saving them for a picnic, refrigerate in a sealed container. Before transport, place them in a 350°F oven for 10-15 minutes until warmed through. Pack in a single layer in a covered, heat-safe baking dish.

Serve to a princess trapped in a tower just before helping her escape to freedom!

Red Riding Hood's Red Fruit Salad

MAKES 4 CUPS (APPROXIMATELY 4 SALADS)

"There was once a sweet little maid, much beloved by everybody, but most of all by her grandmother . . . Once she sent her a little riding hood of red velvet . . . she never wore anything else, people called her 'Little Red Riding Hood.'" — "Little Red Riding Hood"

While most of the fruit in this salad is red, I included some plums and blueberries for visual contrast.

INGREDIENTS

For the Salad
- 8 strawberries
- 1 cup red grapes
- 1 cup fresh cherries
- ½ cup chopped plums
- ½ cup raspberries
- ½ cup blueberries

For the Dressing
- 2 Tbsp pomegranate juice
- 2 tsp fresh lime juice
- 1 tsp honey
- ½ tsp white balsamic vinegar
- ⅛ tsp salt
- ⅛ tsp black pepper

STEP 1. Cut your strawberries, grapes, and cherries in half, discarding the cherry pits.

STEP 2. Add to a medium-sized bowl with the plums, raspberries, and blueberries. Set aside.

STEP 3. Add all dressing ingredients to a small, sealable container and shake vigorously for 1-2 minutes until combined. Drizzle on salad to taste and toss to combine.

Serve to Little Red after defeating the Big Bad Wolf!

Enchanted Swan Cookies

MAKES 8 COOKIES

"Just before the sun went down, Elisa saw eleven white swans with gold crowns on their heads flying towards land. They were gliding across the sky one after the other like a long white ribbon." — "The Wild Swans"

You will need to squeeze pretty firmly to pipe the dough, but if it is too difficult to pipe, trying lightly kneading the outside of the piping bag several times. The heat from your hands should warm and soften the dough, making it easier to pipe.

INGREDIENTS

- **1 cup butter, softened**
- **¾ cup sugar**
- **⅛ tsp salt**
- **1 egg, room temp**
- **1½ tsp vanilla**
- **2 cups flour**
- **2 Tbsp milk, room temp**
- **1 drop yellow gel food coloring**
- **3 drops blue gel food coloring**
- **Black, red, and blue food markers**

NOTE: If your hands get tired during piping, feel free to stop for a few minutes. The dough is very stable, so it won't suffer from sitting for a few extra minutes.

STEP 1. Preheat oven to 350°F. Line 2 baking sheets with parchment paper and set aside. Cream the butter, sugar, and salt in a stand mixer fitted with a paddle attachment on medium speed for 1 minute. Stop to scrape the sides of the bowl. Beat in the egg and vanilla until combined. Reduce speed to medium-low and gradually beat in the flour until combined. Stop and scrape the sides of the bowl. Beat in the milk on medium speed until combined.

STEP 2. Transfer ¼ cup cookie dough to a small bowl and mix in yellow food coloring with a spoon until fully combined. Transfer to a piping bag fitted with a small round tip (such as a Wilton #4). Set aside.

STEP 3. Transfer 1 cup dough to another bowl and mix in blue coloring with a spoon until fully combined. Transfer to a piping bag fitted with a large round tip (such as a Wilton #2A). Set aside.

STEP 4. Transfer ½ cup uncolored dough to a piping bag fitted with a medium round tip (such as a Wilton #12). If desired, pipe a small dot of dough under each corner of the parchment on the baking sheets to keep the parchment in place. Pipe 8 2½-inch squiggles—like a question mark without the dot—on one baking sheet, piping them approximately 3" apart. For each squiggle, start piping at the bottom and curve upward, squeezing for 3 seconds when you reach the end of the curve. This will create the swan head.

Continues on next page.

PRO TIP: For best results, instead of using one swan to make all the indentations, use each swan to make the indentation in the pond you plan to pair with it. The "footprint" of each swan is slightly different, so you'll have better luck getting the swans to stand if you create matching pairs.

STEP 5. Use the yellow dough to pipe a beak and crown onto each swan head. Pipe another layer of dough on top of each crown and beak (this will keep them from being thinner than the rest of the cookie, which helps prevent overbrowning). See top left photo for reference.

STEP 6. Transfer remaining uncolored dough to a piping bag fitted with a large star tip (such as a Wilton #1M). Over the bottom ½" of the swan necks, pipe 8 swan bodies. To make the swan bodies, pipe a 2½" swirl starting from the center and rotating the piping tip outward, then create a tail by continuing to pipe beyond the bottom of the body for about ½", angling the tail slightly upward. If desired, you can pinch the end of the tail to make it taper.

STEP 7. Bake for 10 minutes, rotating the pan halfway through. Allow to cool on the pan for 5 minutes, then use an offset spatula to gently transfer to a wire rack to cool completely. Take care to support the necks, since they are delicate.

STEP 8. While the first sheet of cookies bakes, use the blue dough to pipe 8 2½-inch ovals on the remaining baking sheet, spacing them 1"-2" apart. To pipe the ovals, start in the center and rotate outward. See bottom left photo for reference.

STEP 9. Bake for 10-12 minutes, rotating the pan halfway through. As soon as the blue "ponds" come out of the oven, stand the swans on top, gently pressing down into the ponds to create an indentation in the warm cookie. Set swans aside and allow ponds to cool in the same way as the swans.

STEP 10. Use the black marker to draw eyes on the swans and the red and blue markers to draw gems on the crowns. Store at room temperature in a tightly sealed container. When ready to serve, slot the swans into the top of the ponds. They should stand up.

Serve to some enchanted swans to transform them back into handsome princes!

Poison Apple Punch

MAKES 2½ CUPS

"Snow White longed for the beautiful apple, and as she saw the peasant woman eating a piece of it she could no longer refrain, but stretched out her hand and took the poisoned half." — "Snow White"

This punch can be made either alcoholic or nonalcoholic, depending on your preference.

INGREDIENTS

- 1 cup sparkling or hard apple cider
- ½ cup ginger ale
- ½ cup pomegranate juice
- ¼ cup blood orange bitters
- ¼ cup cranberry juice

STEP 1. Refrigerate all ingredients and combine in a large pitcher. Pour into ½ cup glasses.

Serve to Snow White after trying a glass of it yourself . . . just to make sure it's not poisoned, of course! ;)

Jane Austen

Not only was Jane Austen a brilliant novelist, she was also a passionate foodie. She made her own mead and spruce beer, and she once declared in a letter that she loved Bath buns so much she could live on them! This picnic includes a modernized recipe for Bath buns, along with several recipes inspired by Austen's books—including Regency bride cake!

Mini Bath Buns 46

Mini "Pigeon" Pies 48

Strawberry Fool in a Jar 51

Regency Bride Cake 53

Citrus Mead Punch 54

 # Mini Bath Buns

MAKES 12 BATH BUNS

"They arrived at Bath. Catherine was all eager delight—her eyes were here, there, everywhere, as they approached its fine and striking environs, and afterwards drove through those streets which conducted them to the hotel. She was come to be happy, and she felt happy already." — Northanger Abbey

Bath buns—named for the same city Catherine Morland visits in *Northanger Abbey*—were a popular snack in Regency England and a particular favorite of Jane Austen.

INGREDIENTS

- ¼ cup very warm water
- ½ cup milk, room temperature
- 1 packet (7 grams) active dry yeast
- ¼ cup butter, softened
- ¼ cup sugar
- 1 egg, room temperature
- ½ tsp salt
- 2½ cups plus 2-3 Tbsp flour, divided
- ½ cup raisins or Zante currants
- 2 Tbsp milk
- 5 coarsely crushed sugar cubes

STEP 1. Stir water and milk together in the bowl of a stand mixer. Sprinkle the yeast on top. Stir gently and allow to rest for 5 minutes.

STEP 2. Add the butter, sugar, egg, and salt to the mixer. Beat on medium-low speed with a paddle attachment for 30 seconds or until the butter is broken up into pieces. Gradually beat in 2½ cups of flour. Add the remaining flour 1 tablespoon at a time until dough is soft and pulls away from the bowl. Beat in the raisins until just combined.

STEP 3. Knead on a floured surface for 6-8 minutes. Place dough in a greased bowl, flipping once to coat. Cover and allow to rise for 1 hour in a warm place until doubled in size.

STEP 4. Punch down dough. Cut dough into 12 equal pieces (about 2.4 oz each). Shape each piece into a ball and place them about 2" apart on 2 parchment lined baking sheets. Cover and allow to rise for one more hour. While you wait, preheat oven to 400°F.

Continues on next page.

STEP 5. Brush the tops of the buns with milk. Add crushed sugar to the top of the buns, pressing lightly to adhere. Bake 5 minutes. Flip and rotate the pans. Bake for 5-6 minutes more or until buns are lightly browned on top. Transfer to a wire rack to cool.*

Serve to Jane Austen as a thank you for all her amazing novels!

*If making ahead, top only with milk wash (no sugar). Wrap cooled buns in plastic wrap and tin foil, then freeze. Thaw in wrappings at room temperature for 24 hours. Place thawed buns on a baking sheet lined with parchment paper and brush with milk wash once more. Top with sugar. Bake in a preheated 350°F oven for 5 minutes. Allow to cool on a wire rack.

 # Mini "Pigeon" Pies

MAKES 4 MINI POT PIES

"It was now the middle of June, and the weather fine; and Mrs. Elton was growing impatient to name the day, and settle with Mr. Weston as to pigeon-pies and cold lamb . . ." — Emma

Pigeon pie was a popular meal in Jane Austen's day and is served in *Emma*, but don't worry—these mini pot pies are filled with chicken!

INGREDIENTS

- **1 Tbsp olive oil**
- **⅓ cup each of diced onion, carrot, and celery**
- **1 clove garlic, minced**
- **2 tsp lemon zest**
- **1 tsp snipped fresh sage**
- **¼ tsp ground ginger**
- **½ tsp salt**
- **¼ tsp pepper**
- **1 Tbsp flour**
- **½ cup mead**
- **¼ cup chicken broth**
- **¼ cup milk**
- **4 cups cooked shredded chicken**
- **1 sheet puff pastry dough, thawed**
- **1 egg**
- **1 Tbsp water**
- **1½" heart cookie cutter**

STEP 1. Preheat oven to 350°F. Add oil to a large skillet over medium-low heat. When oil is hot, add the onion, carrot, celery, garlic, lemon zest, sage, ginger, salt, and pepper. Cook for about 3-5 minutes, stirring regularly, until onion is translucent. Add flour, stirring for 1 minute until pasty.

STEP 2. Increase heat to medium. Gradually stir in mead and chicken broth. Bring to a simmer, then cook for 1 more minute. Gradually stir in the milk. Stir in the shredded chicken. Remove from heat.

STEP 3. On a lightly floured surface, roll puff pastry into a 10" square. Place 4 3.5-inch (7 oz) round ramekins upside down over the puff pastry and cut around the edges of the ramekins. Remove ramekins and turn right side up. Evenly divide filling between the ramekins. Cover with puff pastry circles.

STEP 4. Whisk together the egg and water and brush it over the pastry circles. Use the cookie cutter to cut 8 small hearts from the puff pastry scraps. Partially overlap 2 hearts in the center of each pastry circle. Brush egg wash over the shapes. Prick the tops of the pies several times with a fork.

STEP 5. Evenly space ramekins on a baking sheet and bake for 25-30 minutes or until golden brown on top. Allow to rest on the pan for 10 minutes before serving.

Continues on next page.

STEP 6. If making ahead, allow pies to cool completely. Wrap in plastic wrap and tin foil and freeze. Before reheating, thaw for 24 hours in the refrigerator. Remove coverings and reheat on a baking sheet in a 350°F oven for 30 minutes. If transporting, place hot pies in a large, deep casserole dish and cover with tin foil.

Serve to Mrs. Elton during the excursion to Box Hill!

Strawberry Fool in a Jar

MAKES 4 FOOLS

"'You had better explore to Donwell,' replied Mr. Knightley. 'That may be done without horses. Come, and eat my strawberries. They are ripening fast.' . . . Donwell was famous for its strawberry-beds, which seemed a plea for the invitation: but no plea was necessary . . ." — Emma

Fruit fools were a popular dessert in Jane Austen's day. Eighteenth-century fools were made with custard, while modern versions are made with whipped cream. This strawberry fool recipe is made picnic-friendly by packing the fools in sealed mini mason jars and keeping them in a cooler until ready to serve.

INGREDIENTS

- 2 cups fresh quartered strawberries (plus 4 whole strawberries for garnish)
- 3 Tbsp elderflower liqueur
- 1 Tbsp honey
- a pinch of salt
- 1 cup heavy cream
- ½ tsp vanilla
- 1 Tbsp powdered sugar

STEP 1. Add strawberries to a large bowl and set aside. Whisk together elderflower liqueur, honey, and salt in a small bowl until honey is dissolved. Stir liqueur mix through strawberries until well coated. Cover and refrigerate for 30 minutes.

STEP 2. Add heavy cream and vanilla to a stand mixer fitted with a whisk attachment and mix on medium speed for 1-2 minutes until soft peaks form. Turn off mixer. Sift in powdered sugar and mix until stiff peaks form, about 30 seconds. This should yield 2½ cups of whipped cream.

STEP 3. In an 8 oz sealable mason jar, layer ¼ cup each of whipped cream, strawberries, and whipped cream again. Place fresh strawberries on top for garnish. Screw on the lids and refrigerate until ready to serve. If transporting, store in a cooler with ice.

Serve to Emma after an afternoon of strawberry picking at Donwell Abbey!

Regency Bride Cake

MAKES 1 9" LOAF CAKE

"The next variation which their visit afforded was produced by the entrance of servants with cold meat, cake, and a variety of all the finest fruits in season . . . There was now employment for the whole party; for though they could not all talk, they could all eat . . ." — Pride and Prejudice

No Jane Austen menu would be complete without wedding cake. This cake is a modernized, simplified interpretation of a traditional late-1700s bride cake, similar to what would be served at a Regency wedding. Bride cakes were usually large, dense, and filled with dried fruit, candied peel, and nuts. The only raising agent is beaten egg whites, so it's important to fold them in slowly and gently to ensure a good rise.

INGREDIENTS

- **2 cups flour**
- **2 tsp lemon zest**
- **2 tsp orange zest**
- **½ tsp nutmeg**
- **½ tsp allspice**
- **1 cup butter**
- **¾ cup brown sugar, packed**
- **3 eggs**
- **3 Tbsp brandy**
- **1½ cups Zante currants or raisins**
- **½ cup sliced almonds**

STEP 1. Preheat oven to 300°F. Coat a 9" loaf pan with vegetable shortening. Sprinkle the inside liberally with flour. Rotate the pan to coat evenly. Tap out the excess. Set aside.

STEP 2. In a medium bowl, whisk together the flour, lemon zest, orange zest, nutmeg, and allspice. Set aside. In a large bowl, cream the butter with a hand mixer on medium-low speed, then gradually beat in the sugar. Set aside.

STEP 3. Divide the egg whites and yolks. Whisk the egg whites in a bowl on medium speed until stiff peaks form and set aside. In a small bowl, whisk the egg yolks with a fork until smooth and beat into the butter mix. Then beat in the brandy.

STEP 4. Fold the flour mix into the butter mix. Fold in the egg whites until you don't see any streaks (this may take some time, since the dough is dense). Fold in the currants and almonds.

STEP 5. Transfer mix to the prepared loaf pan and spread until even. Bake for 70 minutes until a toothpick inserted in the center comes out clean. Allow to cool in the pan for 10 minutes, then transfer to a wire rack to cool completely.

Serve to any of the lovely brides from Jane Austen's novels!

Citrus Mead Punch

MAKES APPROXIMATELY 6 SERVINGS

"We hear now that there is to be no honey this year. Bad news for us. We must husband our present stock of mead, and I am sorry to perceive that our twenty gallons is very nearly out. I cannot comprehend how the fourteen gallons could last so long."
— Jane Austen, to Cassandra Austen, September 8, 1816

Punch was a necessity at Regency balls, and this punch is inspired by Jane Austen's love of mead-making! Austen was an enthusiastic winemaker, and her family mead recipe is still available today. If you're feeling ambitious, you can use it to make your own mead for this punch!

INGREDIENTS

- 4 cups mead, chilled
- 2¼ cups orange juice, chilled
- 6 Tbsp amaretto, chilled

STEP 1. Combine all ingredients in a large pitcher and stir to combine.

Serve at an elegant Regency ball!

Little Women

Step into the world of the March sisters! This picnic includes Meg's blanc mange with strawberries, Amy's beloved pickled limes, and a more portable version of Jo's corned beef and potatoes—shredded corned beef sandwiches on potato rolls. Wash it all down with some fresh plum iced tea inspired by Plumfield, Aunt March's House.

Orchard House Salad 59

Jo's Corned Beef & Potato Roll Sandwiches . . 60

Pickled Limes with Dried Fruit 62

Blanc Mange with Strawberries 65

Plumfield Iced Tea 67

Orchard House Salad

MAKES 4 SMALL SALADS

". . . Mr. March mildly observed, 'salad was one of the favorite dishes of the ancients, and Evelyn . . .' Here a general explosion of laughter cut short the 'history of salads', to the great surprise of the learned gentleman."

Orchard House was the home of Louisa May Alcott. It was also the inspiration for the March home in *Little Women*. It was named for the property's 12-acre apple orchard. This salad includes not only apples, but also blackberries, almonds, goat cheese and roasted grapes.

INGREDIENTS

For the Salad
- 1 cup red grapes
- 1 Tbsp olive oil
- a pinch of salt
- a pinch of pepper
- ½ an apple, cut into ¼"-thick slices
- 3 cups chopped green lettuce
- ¼ cup blackberries
- ¼ cup crumbled goat cheese
- ¼ cup sliced almonds, toasted

For the Dressing
- 1 Tbsp olive oil
- ½ Tbsp apple juice
- 2 tsp white vinegar
- 1 tsp honey
- a pinch of salt
- a pinch of fresh black pepper

STEP 1. To roast the grapes, preheat oven to 400°F. Add the grapes to a medium bowl with the olive oil, salt, and pepper. Stir until grapes are well coated. Spread on a baking sheet and roast for 8-10 minutes until grapes are soft and slightly wilted. Allow to come to room temperature on the pan.

STEP 2. Combine all salad ingredients in a large bowl and set aside. In a small sealable container, combine all dressing ingredients and shake vigorously for 30 seconds. Drizzle dressing onto salad and toss to combine. Evenly divide between 4 small serving plates.

Serve to the residents of Orchard House!

Jo's Corned Beef & Potato Roll Sandwiches

MAKES 12 SANDWICHES

"'You'd better see what you have got before you think of having company,' said Meg, when informed of the hospitable but rash act. 'Oh, there's corned beef and plenty of potatoes, and I shall get some asparagus and a lobster, 'for a relish', as Hannah says. . .'"

These corned beef and potato roll sandwiches are perfectly portable—just right for a picnic! The best part is you can make both the beef and rolls ahead of time and freeze them (freezing/thawing instructions are included at the end of the recipe).

INGREDIENTS

For the Potato Rolls
- ¼ cup very warm water
- 1 packet (7 grams) active dry yeast
- ½ cup mashed potatoes (about 1 small russet potato with no salt or fat added)
- ½ cup milk
- ¼ cup butter
- ¼ cup sugar
- 1 egg, room temperature
- ½ tsp salt
- 3 cups flour, divided

For the Corned Beef
- 4½ lb beef brisket
- 4 cloves garlic, crushed
- 2 bay leaves
- 2 Tbsp pickling spice

STEP 1. For the potato rolls, add the water to the bowl of a stand mixer. Sprinkle the yeast on top. Give a gentle stir and allow to rest for 5 minutes.

STEP 2. Add the mashed potatoes, milk, and butter to a 2-cup glass liquid measuring cup and microwave for 30 second intervals, stirring between each round of heating, until the butter is fully melted and the mix is warm but not hot. Whisk in the sugar, egg, and salt.

STEP 3. Add the potato mix to the bowl with the yeast. Add half the flour and beat on medium-low speed with a paddle attachment until combined. Gradually beat in the rest of the flour. The dough should be soft and pull away from the bowl.

STEP 4. Knead on a floured surface for 6-8 minutes. Place the dough in a greased bowl, flipping once to coat. Cover and allow to rise for 1 hour in a warm place until doubled.

STEP 5. Preheat oven to 400°F. Punch down dough. Cut dough into 12 equal pieces (about 2.6 oz each). Shape each piece into a ball and place them about 2" apart on a parchment lined baking sheet. Cover and allow to rise for one more hour. As they rise, they will expand enough to touch each other. This is normal and should not be corrected.

Continues on next page.

STEP 6. Bake 10 minutes until rolls are golden brown on top and spring back when tapped with a finger. Transfer to a wire rack to cool by lifting the parchment paper onto the rack, then slide the parchment out from underneath the rolls.

STEP 7. For the corned beef, add the brisket, garlic, and bay leaves to a slow cooker. Sprinkle on pickling spice. Add just enough water to cover the brisket (approximately 3 cups). Cover and cook on low for 8 hours.

Step 8. To assemble, slice the potato rolls widthwise. Shred the beef with 2 forks and place ½ cup between each sliced roll.

STEP 9. If making ahead, you can freeze the cooked brisket and baked rolls in separate sealed containers. Thaw in the refrigerator for about 24 hours. Before serving (or transferring to a container for transport to the picnic), reheat the corned beef in a saucepan over medium heat for 5-10 minutes, stirring regularly.

Serve to Laurie during his next visit to the March house!

Pickled Limes with Dried Fruit

MAKES 8 SERVINGS

"Why, I owe at least a dozen pickled limes, and I can't pay them, you know, till I have money, for Marmee forbade my having anything charged at the shop."

Pickled limes take four weeks to cure. The flavor is a bit less briny than a traditional pickle but more salty, with a mild citrus taste. It pairs well with spiced nuts and dried fruit.

INGREDIENTS

For the Pickled Limes
- **4 limes**
- **¼ cup kosher salt**
- **extra lime juice, approximately 15 oz**

For the Spiced Pecans and Dried Fruit
- **2 Tbsp olive oil**
- **¼ tsp cardamom**
- **¼ tsp ginger**
- **¼ tsp salt**
- **1 cup chopped pecans**
- **½ cup chopped dates**
- **½ cup chopped figs**

STEP 1. For the pickled limes, thoroughly rinse and dry the limes. Cut a deep "X" into each lime, stopping about ¼" from the bottom of the lime. Pack each "X" with kosher salt. Rub additional salt on the outside of each lime. Place the limes in a 4-cup clean glass mason jar. Press the limes with a clean spoon to encourage them to release juice. Seal closed for 2 days, pressing 2 times per day and occasionally shaking the jar to coat the limes in juice.

STEP 2. After 2 days, rinse the salt from the inside and outside of the limes (do not dump out the liquid in the jar). Return the limes to the jar. Fill with enough additional lime juice to fully submerge the limes. Seal closed and refrigerate for 1 month. If a lime bobs to the top of the juice, push it back down with a clean spoon to keep it submerged. When the month is up, lightly rinse limes with clean, cold water and cut into wedges.

STEP 3. For the spiced pecans and dried fruit, preheat oven to 325°F. In a medium bowl, whisk together the olive oil, cardamom. ginger, and salt. Add the pecans and stir until evenly coated. Spread evenly on an ungreased baking sheet and place in the oven for 5-7 minutes or until lightly browned, stirring once halfway through. Allow to cool on the pan. Transfer to a sealed container until ready to use.

Continues on next page.

Step 4. To serve, toss the spiced pecans with the chopped dates and figs. Evenly divide between 8 small serving bowls. Place 2 lime wedges in each bowl.

Serve to Amy March when her teacher makes her throw away her own pickled limes!

Blanc Mange with Strawberries

MAKES 1 8" BLANC MANGE

"... We'll have lettuce and make a salad. I don't know how, but the book tells. I'll have blanc mange and strawberries for dessert, and coffee too, if you want to be elegant."

Blanc mange was a popular dessert during the Civil War, and in *Little Women*, Meg is known to make a particularly good one. Some blanc manges are custards, but this version is set with cornstarch, making it a bit easier to make.

INGREDIENTS

- 4 cups milk
- 1 cup half and half
- ½ cup cornstarch
- ¾ cup sugar
- 1 tsp almond extract
- 3 drops pastel pink gel food coloring
- 1 cup strawberries, quartered (plus more for serving, if desired)
- 2 tsp small mint leaves, optional

NOTE: Measuring ingredients beforehand it always a good idea when cooking, but it's especially important in this recipe. Once you add the cornstarch slurry, you won't be able to step away to measure sugar and such. You'll need to whisk quickly and continuously or the blanc mange could wind up lumpy and not set properly.

STEP 1. Coat the inside of an 8" bundt pan with cooking spray and set aside. In a medium saucepan, bring the milk to a simmer over medium-high heat, swirling the pan occasionally. While you wait, whisk the half and half with the cornstarch to make a slurry.

STEP 2. When the milk simmers, turn the heat down to low. Give the cornstarch slurry a quick stir to ensure no cornstarch has settled to the bottom. Gradually pour the cornstarch slurry into the milk while whisking vigorously. Whisk in the sugar, almond extract, and food coloring. Continue to whisk for 5 minutes. The mix will thicken considerably.

STEP 3. Pour the mix into the prepared tube pan. Allow to come to room temperature (this will take about 2 hours). Refrigerate overnight.

STEP 4. Turn the tube pan over onto a serving plate to release the blanc mange. Fill the centre of the blanc mange with strawberries and mint leaves. If desired, serve with extra strawberries.

Serve at the next March family gathering!

Plumfield Iced Tea

MAKES 6 CUPS ICED TEA

". . . They found they had cause for rejoicing, for she had left Plumfield to Jo, which made all sorts of joyful things possible."

Plumfield, the home of Aunt March, is described as having its own orchards, most likely filled with plum trees. This refreshing plum iced tea would be the perfect beverage to sip in the shade of the plum trees on a hot summer's day.

INGREDIENTS

- **6 cups water**
- **3 tsp whole-leaf cherry black tea**
- **2 tsp whole-leaf blackberry black tea**
- **1 tsp whole-leaf currant black tea**
- **½ a plum, cut into 10 slices**

STEP 1. Heat the water in a kettle until whistling. Steep tea in the hot water in a large bowl or pitcher for 5 minutes. Strain out the tea leaves and refrigerate. Two to three hours before serving, add sliced plums to the pitcher.

STEP 2. When ready to serve, add ice to the pitcher.

Serve to toast Jo when she inherits Plumfield!

Peter Pan

This picnic is perfect for a child's birthday party . . . or for anyone who never wants to grow up! It starts with simple, traditional dishes like ham and cheese pastries, fruit salad, and chocolate cake. Then it adds a touch of whimsy—the pastries are pirate ships, the fruit salad has tropical flavors, and the Fairy Dust Punch has a special surprise!

Peter Hat Chips & Dip 71

Ham and Cheese Pirate Ships 73

Neverland Tropical Fruit Salad 74

Peter's Cake 75

Fairy Dust Punch 79

Peter Hat Chips & Dip

MAKES 24 CHIPS AND 1½ CUPs GUACAMOLE

"She started up with a cry, and saw the boy, and somehow she knew at once that he was Peter Pan . . . He was a lovely boy, clad in skeleton leaves and the juices that ooze out of trees . . ."

Although Peter's iconic hat comes from the movie rather than the book, it's the perfect shape for homemade tortilla chips!

INGREDIENTS

For the Chips
- 2 10" tomato tortillas
- 4 10" spinach tortillas
- 2 Tbsp olive oil
- ⅜ tsp salt

For the Guacamole
- 2 medium avocados, ripe
- ¼ cup chopped red bell pepper
- ¼ cup chopped red onion
- ¼ cup fresh corn
- 1 clove garlic, minced
- 2 fresh basil leaves, snipped
- 1½ tsp lime juice
- ½ tsp ground cumin
- ¼ tsp sea salt
- ⅛ tsp fresh black pepper

STEP 1. To make the chips, start by preheating the oven to 350°F. Cut 24 narrow feather shapes from the tomato tortillas, similar to the one pictured on the next page. Each feather should be about 3" long. Cut several short slits in the edges of each feather. Taper one end more than the other, as with a real feather. This way, when the feather is inserted in the slot in the hat, the tapering can be seen from both ends. If desired, cut a template from paper to use for the first feather, then use that feather as a template for the others.

STEP 2. With a small knife, cut 24 triangles from the spinach tortillas. The long side of each triangle should be 4 ½", while the shorter sides are 3". If desired, you can cut a triangle from the corner of a piece of paper and use that as a stencil.

STEP 3. Cut a horizontal line through each triangle about 5/8" from the bottom. Be careful to leave about ¼" between each end of the line and the outside edges of the triangle. Otherwise, the triangle can tear when the feather is inserted.

Step 4. Insert the feathers into the slots at an angle, so they are resting on one side of the slot. Space the hats evenly apart on 2 ungreased baking sheets (more hats will fit on each baking sheet if you turn every other hat upside down). Brush with olive oil. Sprinkle salt on the hats and toast in the oven for 6-8 minutes, flipping and rotating the pans halfway through. Set on a wire rack to cool.

Continues on next page.

STEP 5. To make the guacamole, peel and seed the avocados. Coarsely chop and place in a medium bowl. Coarsely mash with a potato masher or the bottom of a heavy glass. Add all other guacamole ingredients to the bowl with the avocado. Stir to combine. Add more seasonings to taste, if needed.

STEP 6. If desired, the chips can be made ahead and stored in a sealed plastic bag at room temperature for up to 2 days.

Serve to the Boy Who Would Never Grow Up!

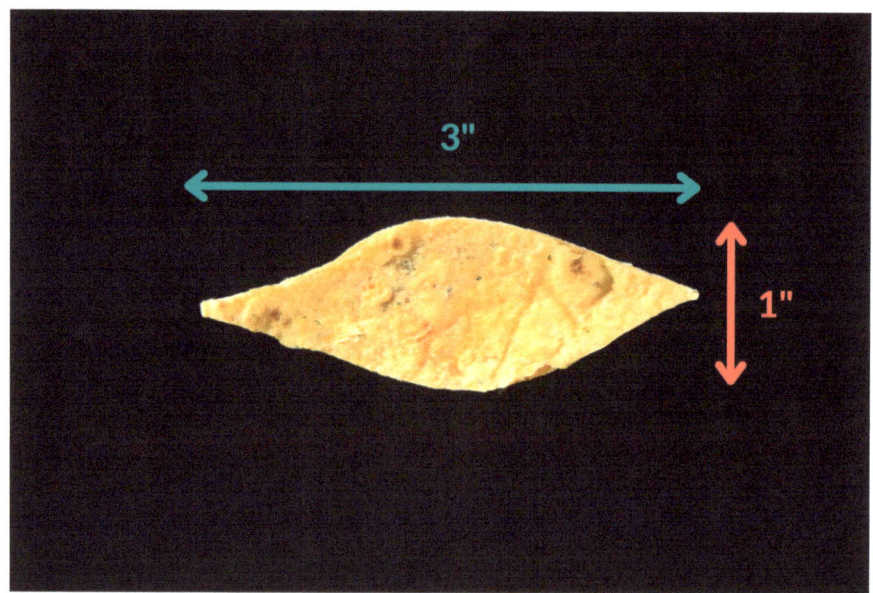

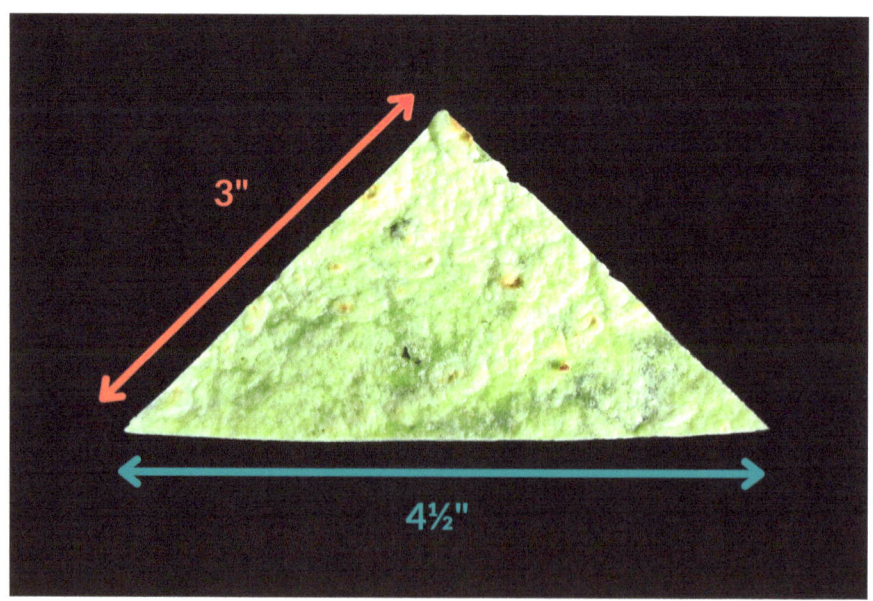

Ham and Cheese Pirate Ships

MAKES 8 PIRATE SHIPS

"One green light squinting over Kidd's Creek, which is near the mouth of the pirate river, marked where the brig, the Jolly Roger, lay, low in the water; a rakish-looking craft foul to the hull . . ."

Hoist the sails! These pirate ship pastries are the perfect alternative to ham and cheese sandwiches. They would also be great for a Peter Pan birthday party—quick to make and just the right size for little hands.

INGREDIENTS

- **1 sheet puff pastry dough, thawed**
- **4 slices deli ham**
- **½ cup shredded Cheddar cheese**
- **1 egg**
- **1 Tbsp water**
- **8 pirate flag cocktail toothpicks**

STEP 1. Preheat oven to 400°F. On a floured surface, roll out the dough to an 11" x 14" rectangle. Cut 8 4" circles from the dough, gathering and rerolling the dough if needed. Cut the ham slices in half and place them on the bottom half of each circle, leaving a ¼" of the dough exposed at the bottom (this will give the top something to adhere to when folded).

STEP 2. Evenly divide the cheese among the circles, placing it on top of the ham. Whisk the egg with the water in a small bowl and brush it onto the edges of the circles. Fold the top of the circles over the filling and press the edges closed with a fork.

STEP 3. Space the pastries evenly apart on a greased baking sheet. Brush egg wash on top and prick the top of each pastry with a fork. Bake for 10-15 minutes or until golden on top. Transfer to a wire rack to cool. Insert a pirate flag in the flat edge of each pastry. If making ahead, freeze in a sealed container. Thaw in the refrigerator for 24 hours, then reheat at 350°F for 5 minutes (do not insert flags until after reheating).

Serve to the pirates of the Jolly Roger!

Neverland Tropical Fruit Salad

MAKES 4 SALADS

"Neverland is always more or less an island, with astonishing splashes of colour here and there, and coral reefs and rakish-looking craft in the offing. . . and either these are part of the island or they are another map showing through, and it is all rather confusing, especially as nothing will stand still."

Bring the tropical flavors of Neverland to life with dragon fruit, mango, and of course some star fruit! Don't forget to sprinkle on some chili lime seasoning for extra kick.

INGREDIENTS

- **2 dragon fruit**
- **2" star cookie cutter**
- **½ cup mango, cubed**
- **½ cup pineapple, cubed**
- **1 starfruit, sliced into ¼"-thick stars**
- **1 kiwi fruit, peeled and sliced into ¼"-thick disks**
- **½ cup red grapes, sliced in half**
- **Chili lime seasoning, to taste**

STEP 1. Cut dragon fruit in half lengthwise. Scoop out each half in one piece using a spoon. Cut each scoop into ¼" thick planks and cut out stars using a 2" star cookie cutter.

STEP 2. Evenly divide all the fruit between the hollowed-out dragon fruit, placing the starfruit and dragon fruit stars on top. Sprinkle on chili lime seasoning.

Serve to the Darling children when they arrive in Neverland!

NOTE: If you make a double batch of salad or are serving it buffet-style, you can use the pineapple halves as bowls instead of the dragon fruit.

Peter's Cake

MAKES 1 2-LAYER, 6" CAKE

". . cook a large rich cake of a jolly thickness with green sugar on it. . .We will leave the cake on the shore of the Mermaids' Lagoon. . .They will find the cake and they will gobble it up, because, having no mother, they don't know how dangerous 'tis to eat rich damp cake."

If you're new to cake decorating, a great way to keep it simple is to keep the piping to a minimum and decorate with add-ons like candy, sprinkles, and cupcake toppers.

INGREDIENTS

For the Cake
- ¾ cup flour
- ¾ cup cocoa powder
- ¾ tsp baking powder
- ⅜ tsp baking soda
- ⅜ tsp salt
- 6 Tbsp butter, softened
- 1 cup sugar
- 1½ tsp vanilla
- 3 eggs, room temp
- 4 Tbsp sour cream
- 1 tsp distilled white vinegar
- ¾ cup buttermilk

For the Frosting
- 4½ cups powdered sugar
- 1 cup butter, softened
- 20 drops (approximately ¼ tsp) green gel food coloring
- ¼ cup milk, divided
- 2 tsp vanilla

For the Decorations
- "Never Grow Up" cake topper
- 6 gold star cake toppers
- 8 chocolate gold coins

STEP 1. For the cake, preheat oven to 350°F. Coat 2 6" cake pans with cooking spray and line the bottoms with 6" parchment paper circles. Coat the tops of the parchment circles with cooking spray. Set pans aside.

STEP 2. Whisk together all the dry ingredients in a medium bowl and set aside. Cream the butter on medium speed in a large bowl. Beat in the sugar and vanilla until combined. Then beat in the eggs one at a time. Beat in the sour cream and vinegar. Beat in half the dry mix, then half the buttermilk. Alternate beating in remaining dry mix and buttermilk.

STEP 3. Divide the batter evenly between the pans and bake for 30-35 minutes until the tops of the cakes spring back when firmly tapped with a finger. Allow to rest in the pan for 5 minutes. Loosen edges with a knife and remove from pan to a wire rack to cool.

STEP 4. For the frosting, sift the powdered sugar into a medium bowl and set aside. Beat the butter on medium speed in a standing mixer until smooth. Beat in 2 cups of the powdered sugar and beat until combined, stopping to scrape the sides of the bowl if necessary. Stir the food coloring into the milk until well combined. Beat the vanilla and 2 tablespoons of milk into the butter mix. Alternate beating in the remaining powdered sugar and milk.

Step 5. Level off the cake layers. Before you begin decorating, reserve 1 cup of frosting.

Continues on next page.

NOTE: If making ahead, freeze the frosted cake for 1-2 hours, then wrap in 3 layers of plastic wrap. Freeze for 2-3 weeks. At least 24 hours before serving, unwrap the cake and transfer to the refrigerator. Transfer to counter 3 hours before serving.

STEP 6. Place 1 layer cut side up on a turntable or serving plate. Spread a layer of frosting ½" thick over the top of the layer (approximately ½ cup). Place another layer cut side down on top. Using approximately 1 cup of frosting, spread a very thin layer of frosting over the outside of the cake and refrigerate until firm (this is called the "crumb coat" and will help prevent cake crumbs from getting into the final layer of frosting).

STEP 7. Spread more frosting in an even layer over the top and sides of the cake. Add reserved frosting to a piping bag fitted with a large star tip (such as a Wilton #1M). Evenly space 6 swirls of frosting around the top edge of the cake. Pipe a larger, taller swirl in the center. If decorating directly on a serving plate, pipe stars along the bottom edge. If decorating on a turntable, add the stars after transferring to the serving plate.

STEP 8. Add the chocolate coins around the outside of the cake, pressing gently to adhere. Insert cake toppers.

Serve to Peter Pan to celebrate defeating Captain Hook!

Fairy Dust Punch

MAKES 4 SERVINGS

"Of course Peter had been trifling with them, for no one can fly unless the fairy dust has been blown on him. Fortunately, as we have mentioned, one of his hands was messy with it, and he blew some on each of them, with the most superb results."

This punch recipe has a special surprise—cotton candy glitter bombs! Just add a ball of cotton candy filled with luster dust to each glass and watch your drink sparkle with fairy dust.

INGREDIENTS

- **1 quart lemon-lime soda, chilled**
- **3 cups grapefruit juice, chillled**
- **2 cups pineapple juice, chilled**
- **½ cup pink cotton candy, packed**
- **1 tsp white luster dust**

STEP 1. Combine soda, grapefruit juice and pineapple juice in a large pitcher. Evenly divide between 4 16-oz glasses.

STEP 2. Divide cotton candy into 4 equal portions. Pour ¼ tsp luster dust in the center of each portion. Press each portion into a ball, enclosing the luster dust inside. Place in a tightly sealed plastic bag until ready to serve. If it's a hot day, you may want to add the cotton candy balls right way, or the cotton candy could begin to dissolve from humidity in the air.

STE 3. When ready to serve, add a cotton candy ball to each glass and stir until dissolved.

Serve while thinking happy thoughts!

NOTE: Serve in clear glass or plastic cups with a straw. The clear cup makes it easier to see the effect of the luster dust, and the straw makes it easier to stir in the cotton candy and make the luster dust swirl again once it settles.

Peter Rabbit

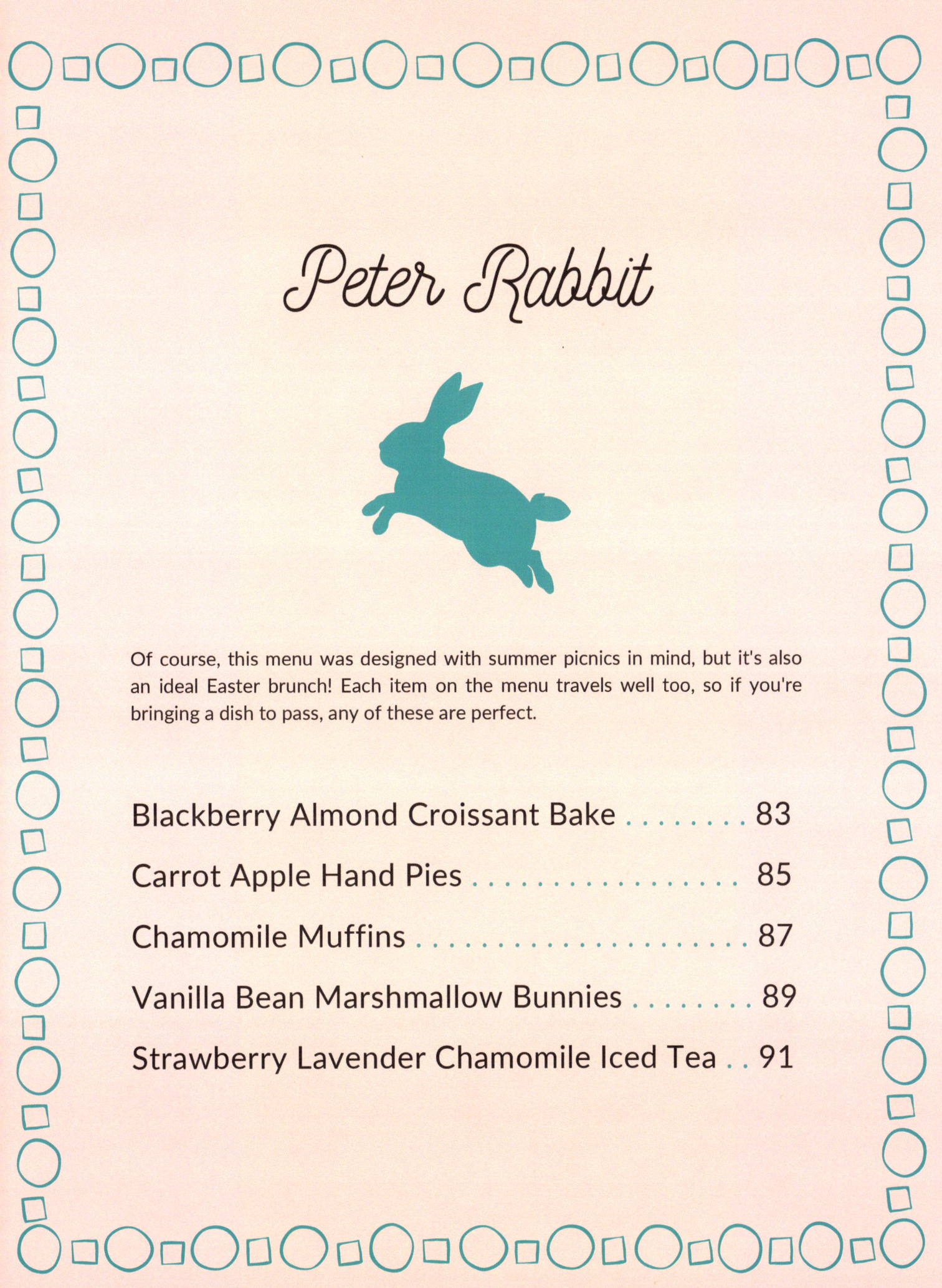

Of course, this menu was designed with summer picnics in mind, but it's also an ideal Easter brunch! Each item on the menu travels well too, so if you're bringing a dish to pass, any of these are perfect.

Blackberry Almond Croissant Bake 83

Carrot Apple Hand Pies 85

Chamomile Muffins 87

Vanilla Bean Marshmallow Bunnies 89

Strawberry Lavender Chamomile Iced Tea . . 91

Blackberry Almond Croissant Bake

MAKES 1 9"x13" CROISSANT BAKE

"But Flopsy, Mopsy, and Cottontail had bread and milk and blackberries for supper."

If you want to make your own almond butter for this bake, check out my recipe for Card Suit Tea Sandwiches (p. 12).

STEP 1. Preheat oven to 350°F. Spread the croissant pieces in an even layer on the bottom of a 9" x 13" glass or ceramic baking dish. Scatter the blackberries and almonds on top. Set aside.

STEP 2. In a large bowl, beat the cream cheese until fluffy. Beat in the honey until well combined, then the almond butter. Beat in the eggs, stopping to scrape the sides of the bowl if necessary. Beat in the milk, lemon zest, and salt, paying special attention to the sides and bottom of the bowl.

STEP 3. Pour the cream cheese mix in an even layer over the contents of the baking dish.

STEP 4. Bake for 40 minutes or until set in the center and golden brown on top. Remove from oven.

STEP 5. If serving right away, allow to cool for 10 minutes before eating. If saving for later, store covered in the refrigerator. Reheat in a 350°F oven for 10-15 minutes until warmed through, then cover with tin foil until ready to serve.

Serve warm to Flopsy, Mopsy, and Cottontail for being good little bunnies.

INGREDIENTS

- 12 mini croissants, cut into quarters
- 2 cups frozen blackberries
- ¼ cup sliced almonds
- 8 oz cream cheese, softened
- ½ cup honey
- ¼ cup almond butter
- 2 eggs
- 1 cup milk
- Zest of 1 lemon
- ½ tsp salt

Carrot Apple Hand Pies

MAKES 8-9 HAND PIES

"'Now my dears,' said old Mrs. Rabbit one morning, 'you may go into the fields or down the lane, but don't go into Mr. McGregor's garden.'"

Can't have a rabbit-inspired menu without a carrot recipe! These delicious pies are filled with a blend of carrot, apple, and ginger. And they're shaped like little bunnies too! They're almost too cute to eat . . . Almost! ;)

INGREDIENTS

- 3 cups flour
- 2 tsp salt
- 1 cup plus 2 Tbsp unsalted butter, cut into cubes
- ½-¾ cup ice water
- 3 medium carrots, peeled and chopped
- 1 Pink Lady apple, peeled, seeded, and chopped
- ½ onion, diced
- 3 tsp fresh ginger, grated
- 2 Tbsp olive oil
- 1 tsp ground sage
- ½ tsp salt
- ¼ tsp pepper
- ½ cup heavy cream
- 2 Tbsp flour
- 4" bunny head cookie cutter
- 1 egg

*Alternatively, you can put the flour-salt mix in a food processor with most of the butter, process on low for 30-60 seconds, then add remaining butter and process for 15 seconds or until desired texture is reached. It requires transferring back to the large bowl for the water stage, but it's faster.

STEP 1. In a large bowl, stir together the flour and salt. Cut in the butter with a fork until it has a sandy texture with pea-sized bits scattered throughout.* Add water a few tablespoons at time, stirring with a fork, until mix is shaggy and damp (but not wet) and holds together when pressed. Shape into a ball. Separate into 2 smaller balls of equal size and flatten into 6" disks. Wrap tightly in plastic wrap and refrigerate for at least 30 minutes.

STEP 2. Preheat oven to 375°F. Add carrots, apple, onion, ginger, olive oil, sage, salt, and pepper to a large bowl. Stir to combine. Spread out on a greased baking sheet. Cook for 25-30 minutes or until soft, stirring halfway through. Puree in a blender with the cream. Transfer to a saucepan over medium heat. Add flour and cook for 2-3 minutes, stirring continuously. Set aside.

STEP 3. Increase oven temperature to 400°F. Line a baking sheet with parchment paper and set side. Roll out the first dough disk to ¼" thickness and use a 4" bunny head cookie cutter to cut out 5 bunnies. Gather and reroll the scraps, then cut 3-4 more bunnies. Place evenly apart on the baking sheet. Add approximately 1 Tbsp filling to the center of each bunny and 1 tsp of filling in the ears (it may be easier to shape the mix with your hands than spoon it on). See first photo on next page for reference. Roll out remaining dough disk and cut 8-9 more bunnies, gathering and rerolling the scraps as needed. Rotate each bunny between your fingers, pinching the edges to make them thinner on the ends than in the center.

Continues on next page.

STEP 4. Whisk egg with 1 Tbsp water and brush around the edges of the bunnies on the pan. Place the new bunnies on top of the filled bunnies, pressing down around the edges to adhere. Crimp the edges with a fork. Brush the tops with egg wash. Using a chopstick or toothpick, poke three holes in each bunny to make a face, rotating the chopstick to widen each hole. See bottom photo for reference.

STEP 5. Bake for 25 minutes until golden on top. Transfer to a wire rack to cool completely. Refrigerate in a sealed container. If saving them for a picnic, reheat them in a 350°F oven for 10 minutes before transporting. Pack in a single layer in a covered, heat-safe baking dish.

Serve to Mr. McGregor after he chases away a mischievous rabbit.

Chamomile Muffins

MAKES 12 MUFFINS

"His mother put him to bed, and made some chamomile tea. She gave a dose of it to Peter! 'One tablespoonful to be taken at bedtime,' she said."

Chamomile pairs perfectly with baked goods, making it an excellent addition to this healthy muffin recipe. Not only are they easy to pack for a picnic, they're also an amazing breakfast!

INGREDIENTS

- ½ cup butter
- 2 cups flour
- 2 tsp baking powder
- ⅛ tsp salt
- 2 chamomile teabags
- 1 brown banana
- ¼ cup honey
- ¼ cup milk
- ¼ cup strong chamomile tea, room temperature*
- ¼ cup sugar
- 2 tsp vanilla
- 1 egg

*Make the tea strong by steeping 1 teabag in ¼ cup hot water for 4 minutes. After refrigerating, check the water level to make sure too much didn't evaporate out. Add extra water if needed.

STEP 1. Preheat oven to 375°F. Melt the butter and set aside, allowing it to come to room temperature. Fill a muffin tin with liners and set aside.

STEP 2. In a large bowl, whisk together the flour, baking powder, and salt. Cut open the tea bags and whisk the tea leaves into the flour mix. Discard the empty bags.

STEP 3. In a medium bowl, mash the banana. Add the honey, milk, chamomile tea, sugar, and vanilla. Whisk with a fork until combined. Whisk in the butter, then the egg. Pour the wet ingredients into the dry all at once and whisk with the fork until just combined.

STEP 4. Evenly divide the batter between the cupcake liners and bake for 20-25 minutes, until muffins are cracked on top and spring back when firmly tapped with a finger. Transfer to a wire rack to cool.

Serve as a delightful summer snack!

Vanilla Bean Marshmallow Bunnies

MAKES 8 BUNNIES

"Once upon a time there were four little Rabbits, and their names were: Flopsy, Mopsy, Cottontail, and Peter."

If you're new to making piped marshmallows and want to make this recipe for a party, I recommend practicing it a couple times first. Light, even pressure is really important to piping smooth, consistent marshmallow shapes, which is best learned with practice.

INGREDIENTS

- ½ cup cornstarch
- ½ cup powdered sugar
- 1 Tbsp gelatin powder
- ¼ cup plus 2 Tbsp cold water
- ¾ cup sugar
- ¼ cup room temperature water
- ¼ cup plus 2 Tbsp corn syrup
- a pinch of salt
- 4 Tbsp pasteurized egg whites
- 1 vanilla bean, split
- 1 drop pink gel food coloring
- 6 drops black gel food coloring

NOTE: Piped marshmallow sets as it cools. Once your mix is ready, you won't be able to step away and come back to it later. So once you start working, make sure you can complete the recipe uninterrrupted.

STEP 1. Line a baking sheet with parchment paper. Whisk together the cornstarch and powdered sugar and sift half the mix over the parchment paper. Set aside. To a medium bowl, add the gelatin. Gently stir in the cold water and allow to bloom for 10 minutes.

STEP 2. While you wait, add the sugar, room temperature water, corn syrup, and salt to a medium saucepan. Do not stir. Heat on medium-high until the mixture reaches 240°F on a candy thermometer (approximately 7 minutes), swirling the pan occasionally. When there are about 3 minutes left on the timer, add the egg whites to a stand mixer fitted with a whisk attachment and beat on medium speed until soft peaks form.

STEP 3. When the sugar mix reaches 240°F, whisk the gelatin to break it up, then very slowly whisk it into the hot sugar mix. With the mixer running, whisk the sugar-gelatin mix into the egg whites, taking care not to let the sugar mix touch the side of the mixer bowl. Gradually increase the speed to the highest setting and beat until the mixture is white and opaque and the bowl is almost completely cool to the touch (6-7 minutes). While it's beating, scrape in the vanilla seeds. The mix is done when you can use the attachment to swirl a figure eight over the mix and it disappears in about 20 seconds.

Continues on next page.

*After 3-5 days they still taste amazing, but they'll get a bit stale. If that happens, they're great for use in hot chocolate for several weeks.

STEP 4. Transfer 1½ cups marshmallow mix to a piping bag fitted with a Wilton #2A piping tip and pipe 8 3-inch teardrop shapes onto the prepared baking sheet. Keep a small bowl of water nearby and flatten any peaks in the marshmallow with a tap from a wet finger. Pipe a 1" ball over the narrow end of each teardrop. Pipe a tail on the end of each rabbit.

STEP 5. Transfer ½ cup marshmallow mix to a piping bag fitted with a Wilton #10 tip and pipe 2 long hollow teardrop shapes behind each head and over the body to make the ears.

STEP 6. Transfer ½ cup mix to a small, microwaveable bowl and stir in 1 drop pink gel coloring. By this point, your marshmallow mix may be starting to set. If so, put the bowl in the microwave for 5 seconds and stir. You can microwave any portion of the marshmallow mix up to 2 times if needed. Transfer pink mix to a piping bag fitted with a Wilton #4 tip and fill the open space in each ear with pink coloring.

STEP 7. Transfer ¼ cup mix to a small bowl and stir in 6 drops black gel coloring, microwaving if needed. Transfer black mix to a piping bag fitted with a Wilton #2 tip. Pipe eyes and noses onto each bunny.

STEP 8. Allow to set uncovered overnight. Sift remaining sugar-cornstarch mix over the bunnies. Tap excess sugar from the bunnies. To store, transfer the bed of sugar-cornstarch mix to a 9" x 13" storage container lined with wax paper. Place the bunnies on top 1"-2" apart. Cover lightly with a lid or plastic wrap for 3-5 days.* You can also pipe the leftover marshmallow mix into dollops, dust with sugar mix, and store similarly.

Serve to Peter Rabbit to encourage him to stay out of Mr. McGregor's garden.

Strawberry Lavender Chamomile Iced Tea

MAKES 6 CUPS

"His mother put him to bed, and made some chamomile tea. She gave a dose of it to Peter! 'One tablespoonful to be taken at bedtime,' she said."

Have a sip of summer with this refreshing white tea flavored with strawberry, chamomile, and lavender.

INGREDIENTS

- 3 tsp white strawberry tea
- 1½ tsp dried chamomile flowers
- 3 tsp dried lavender flowers
- 1 Tbsp freeze-dried strawberries, broken into pieces

STEP 1. Heat 6 cups water in a tea kettle just until steaming (don't let it whistle). Add water and ingredients to a large pitcher and steep for 5 minutes. Strain out tea leaves and refrigerate until cold. If desired, lightly sweeten with honey before refrigerating.

Serve to Peter as he recovers from his adventure in Mr. McGregor's garden!

The Secret Garden

When I created this menu inspired by *The Secret Garden*, I wanted to make sure every part of the garden was represented: flowers, fruits, vegetables, and herbs! Every bite is light and refreshing, exactly what you need after a hot day of gardening.

Herbed Key Crackers 94

Fruit & Flower Chicken Salad Croissants . . 95

Garden Gate Salad 96

Chocolate Raspberry Cream Puffs 97

Sparkling Rose Lemonade 101

Herbed Key Crackers

MAKES 32 CRACKERS

". . . As she looked she saw something almost buried in the newly turned soil . . . It was an old key which looked as if it had been buried a long time. . .'Perhaps it has been buried for ten years,' she said in a whisper. 'Perhaps it is the key to the garden!'"

The unique key shape gives these darling little crackers added flair with no extra effort.

INGREDIENTS

- 1 cup flour
- ½ tsp baking powder
- 2 tsp fresh rosemary, minced
- ⅜ tsp salt, plus more for sprinkling
- 1 clove garlic, minced
- 5 Tbsp water
- ¼ cup olive oil, plus more for brushing
- 3" key shaped cookie cutter

STEP 1. Place a baking sheet in the oven and set to 450°F. In a large bowl, whisk together the flour, baking powder, rosemary, and salt. Create a well in the center. Set aside.

STEP 2. In a cup or small bowl, whisk together the garlic, water, and olive oil. Pour into the well and whisk with a fork until combined. It will form a loose, soft dough.

STEP 3. Knead the dough for 1 minute on a lightly floured surface until a smooth ball forms. Reflour your surface and roll out dough to 1mm thickness (or as thin as you can get it). Cut out 16 keys with the cookie cutter. Place them 1" apart on the warmed baking sheet.

STEP 4. Prick keys 3 times with a fork and lightly brush with olive oil. Lightly sprinkle with salt. Bake for 8 minutes or until crisped through and golden along the edges. Transfer to a wire rack to cool.

STEP 5. Reroll remaining dough. Cut out 16 more keys and bake as in Step 4. Cool completely and store with wax paper between layers in a tightly sealed container for up to 3 weeks.

Serve at a party in your secret garden!

Fruit & Flower Chicken Salad Croissants

MAKES 6 CROISSANT SANDWICHES

"At first it seemed that green things would never cease pushing their way through the earth . . . and the buds began to unfurl and show color, every shade of blue, every shade of purple, every tint and hue of crimson."

This refreshing alternative to traditional chicken salad features apples, apricots, and a bit of dried chamomile, bringing garden and orchard together for a truly delicious entrée.

INGREDIENTS

- **8 oz mascarpone**
- **2 Tbsp whole milk**
- **½ tsp salt**
- **12½ oz (1 heaping cup) cubed or shredded cooked chicken**
- **¼ Pink Lady apple, chopped**
- **6 dried apricots, chopped**
- **1 tsp dried chamomile flowers**
- **6 croissants**
- **3 green lettuce leaves**

STEP 1. In a small bowl, whisk together the mascarpone, milk, and salt until smooth. Set aside.

STEP 2. In a large bowl, add the chicken, apple, apricots, and chamomile. Add in the mascarpone mix, stirring until well combined. Cover and refrigerate for at least 30 minutes.

STEP 3. Slice croissants in half widthwise. Tear the lettuce leaves in half and use them to line the bottoms of the croissants. Scoop chicken salad on top. Cover tightly with plastic wrap and refrigerate until ready to serve.

Serve while enjoying a garden in full bloom!

Garden Gate Salad

MAKES 6 SALADS

"The secret garden was not the only one Dickon worked in. Round the cottage on the moor there was a piece of ground enclosed by a low wall of rough stones . . . Dickon worked there planting or tending potatoes and cabbages, turnips and carrots and herbs for his mother."

No need for bowls with this salad—they're served in hollowed out bell peppers!

INGREDIENTS

For the Honey Lemon Vinaigrette
- ½ Tbsp white wine vinegar
- ½ Tbsp olive oil
- ½ Tbsp fresh lemon juice
- 2 tsp honey
- ⅛ tsp salt
- ⅛ tsp pepper

For the Salad
- 4 medium red or orange bell peppers
- 6 medium dandelion greens, chopped
- 6 large turnip greens, deveined and chopped
- 3 radishes, sliced into thin coins
- ¼ of an English cucumber, sliced into thin coins
- Freshly grated Parmesan, to taste

STEP 1. In a small, sealable container, combine the white wine vinegar, olive oil, lemon juice, honey, salt, and pepper. Seal container and shake vigorously to combine. Set aside.

STEP 2. Cut 3 bells peppers in half lengthwise (these will be your bowls). Devein and deseed the halves. Set aside. Deseed and dice the remaining bell pepper. Add the diced pepper to a medium bowl with the dandelion greens, turnip greens, radishes, and cucumber. Pour on the dressing and toss to combine. Divide salad mix evenly between bell pepper halves. Top with Parmesan to taste. To save for later, wrap salads individually in plastic wrap and refrigerate until ready to serve.

Serve to celebrate the bounty of summer!

 # Chocolate Raspberry Cream Puffs

MAKES 26 CREAM PUFFS

"What a wonderful thing for Mrs. Sowerby to think of! What a kind, clever woman she must be! How good the buns were! And what delicious fresh milk!"

Though cream puffs don't appear in *The Secret Garden*, all the ingredients do, namely milk, butter, and eggs. I like to imagine that maybe Mrs. Sowerby makes cream puffs sometimes as a special treat. A perfect way to elevate humble ingredients!

INGREDIENTS

For the Pastry Cream
- 2 whole eggs, plus 2 egg yolks
- ½ cup cocoa powder
- ½ cup plus 2 Tbsp sugar
- 3 Tbsp cornstarch
- ½ tsp salt
- 2 cups whole milk

For the Choux Pastry
- ½ cup butter
- 1 cup water
- 1 cup flour
- 4 eggs, thoroughly beaten

For Decoration
- 1 cup powdered sugar
- 2 Tbsp milk
- 1 drop pink gel food coloring
- 26 fresh raspberries
- Extra powdered sugar, for dusting

STEP 1. For the pastry cream, whisk together the eggs, egg yolks, cocoa powder, sugar, cornstarch, and salt in a large mixing bowl with a fork. It will form a shiny paste. Set aside. Add the milk to a large saucepan on medium heat, whisking regularly to prevent a skin and an overcooked bottom. The milk will foam a bit as you whisk. After 5-7 minutes, the milk will begin to foam upward quickly. Turn off heat. Very gradually whisk ½ cup of the heated milk into the egg mix until fully incorporated. Whisk in another ½ cup the same way. Gradually whisk the tempered egg mix into the rest of the milk.

STEP 2. Return to medium heat, whisking constantly for 3 minutes (the mixture will thicken slightly and start to bubble). Whisk for 2 minutes more. The mixture will thicken considerably. Remove from heat and transfer to a sealable container. Whisk while inside the container for 1 minute. Secure lid and refrigerate for at least 90 minutes until cold through, placing a layer of plastic wrap over the pastry cream after 20 minutes, making sure the plastic is in direct contact with the cream (this will prevent the cream from developing a skin).

STEP 3. For the choux pastry, move the racks in your oven to the top and bottom positions. Preheat oven to 400°F. Line two baking sheets with parchment paper or silicone mats and set aside.

Continues on next page.

*If you're prepping ahead and plan to save your cream puffs for another day, don't fill or decorate them until the day they're served. Instead, store pastry shells at room temp in a sealed container and pastry cream covered in the fridge for up to 3 days. You can fill and decorate the shells several hours ahead. Once assembled, refrigerate them before serving.

STEP 4. Melt the butter and water together in a large saucepan on low heat. Turn the heat to medium and bring to a boil. Turn off the heat and pour in the flour all at once. Stir together quickly with a silicone spatula. Turn the heat back to medium. Cook for 2 minutes, stirring constantly. Remove from heat. Transfer mix to a large mixing bowl. Beat in the eggs ½ tablespoon at a time with a hand mixer on medium speed until smooth.

STEP 5. Fit a piping bag with a large round tip (such as a Wilton #2A) and fill the bag with half the pastry dough. Pipe 13 mounds at least 1½" apart on one baking sheet. The mounds should be 1½" across and about 1" high. Refill the bag and pipe 13 mounds on the remaining baking sheet. Place the sheets in the oven. Bake for 20 minutes. Turn the heat down to 350°F; flip and rotate the pans. Bake for 20 minutes more. Turn off the heat and let the pastry shells sit for 10 minutes in the oven. Remove to a wire rack to cool.

STEP 6. Fit a piping bag with a medium round tip (such as a Wilton #12). Stir refrigerated pastry cream with a spoon and transfer to the piping bag. Cut a small "X" with a sharp knife in the bottom of each pastry shell and insert the piping tip through the "X." Fill each pastry shell with cream.

STEP 7. For decoration, whisk the powdered sugar, milk, and food coloring together in a bowl. Spoon a small amount onto each cream puff. Top with fresh raspberries and powdered sugar.*

Serve as the crown jewel of your next summer celebration!

99

Sparkling Rose Lemonade

MAKES APPROXIMATELY 5½ CUPS

"He stopped and lifted his face to look up at the climbing and hanging sprays above him —'there'll be a fountain o' roses here this summer.'"

Subbing out the water for club soda is an easy way to elevate any lemonade recipe.

INGREDIENTS

- 1 cup fresh lemon juice
- 1½ cups simple syrup, divided
- 3 cups cold club soda
- ⅜ tsp rose water, divided
- 6 drops pink gel food coloring

STEP 1. Mix the lemon juice and 1 cup simple syrup in a pitcher until dissolved. Add the club soda slowly (it will fizz upward significantly). Stir in ¼ tsp rose water and the food coloring. Taste and add remaining simple syrup and rose water as desired. Refrigerate until ready to serve.

Serve as the perfect refreshment after a long day of gardening!

Winnie-the-Pooh

These recipes inspired by the Hundred Acre Wood include honey wherever possible, including an array of fruits, vegetables, and nuts. They are all excellent foods to snack on while relaxing in the forest shade, but the Honey Almond Granola Bars and Tigger Stripe Fruit Leather are also healthy hiking snacks!

Honey Almond Granola Bars 104

Rabbit's Garden Wraps 105

Tigger Stripe Fruit Leather 109

Honey Clementine Cupcakes 110

Eeyore's "Feeling Blue" Iced Lattes 113

Honey Almond Granola Bars

MAKES 8 GRANOLA BARS

"Then he thought another long time, and said: 'And the only reason for being a bee that I know of is making honey.' And then he got up, and said: 'And the only reason for making honey is so as I can eat it.' So he began to climb the tree."

This recipe is easy to customize to suit your taste. Feel free to sub in your favorite nuts or dried fruit! If you want to make your own almond butter, check out my recipe on p. 12.

INGREDIENTS

- 1 cup rolled oats
- ¼ cup sliced almonds
- ½ cup crisped rice cereal
- ⅓ cup honey
- ⅓ cup almond butter
- 2 heaping Tbsp chopped dried apricots
- 2 heaping Tbsp dried blueberries
- 2 Tbsp golden raisins

STEP 1. Preheat oven to 325°F. On an ungreased baking sheet, spread out the oats and almonds. Toast for 8-10 minutes or until just beginning to brown, stirring once halfway through. Transfer to a large bowl with the rice cereal and stir together, reserving approximately 2 tsp of almonds.

STEP 2. Microwave the honey for 30-45 seconds until just beginning to bubble. Whisk in the almond butter with a fork until smooth. Transfer to the large bowl and stir until well incorporated. Stir in the apricots, blueberries, and raisins, reserving approximately 1 tsp each of the apricots and blueberries.

STEP 3. Transfer mixture to a 9" x 5" loaf pan lined with parchment paper. Spread evenly in the pan with a spatula. Gently press the reserved almonds, apricots, and blueberries into the top. Press flat, taking care not to crush the almonds. Refrigerate uncovered for 1 hour. Transfer mix to a cutting board and slice into 1" wide bars while cold. Store covered in a single layer at room temp or in the refrigerator.

Serve before heading out for a day of hiking in the Hundred Acre Wood!

Rabbit's Garden Wraps

MAKES 4 WRAPS (8 SERVINGS)

"It was going to be one of Rabbit's busy days. As soon as he woke up he felt important, as if everything depended upon him. It was just the day for Organizing Something, or for Writing a Notice Signed Rabbit, or for seeing What Everybody Else Thought About It."

This recipe uses turnip greens, but if you don't like turnips, never fear! The greens taste nothing like the root. They have a very mild yet hearty vegetal flavor. However, you can sub in spinach or green leaf lettuce if you like!

INGREDIENTS

For the Hummus
- 1 red bell pepper
- 1 clove garlic, minced
- 2 Tbsp olive oil, divided
- ¾ tsp salt, divided
- ¼ cup tahini
- ¼ cup cold water
- 3 Tbsp lemon juice
- 1 can chickpeas, rinsed and drained

For the Tomato Salad
- 4 Roma tomatoes
- ½ red onion
- 1 Tbsp olive oil
- ½ tsp red wine vinegar
- ¼ tsp salt
- ⅛ tsp pepper

For the Cream Cheese
- 8 medium basil leaves
- 8 oz cream cheese, softened

For the Wraps
- 4 10-inch spinach tortillas
- 4 medium turnip greens
- 2 cups cooked quinoa (½ cup when raw), cooled
- 1 English cucumber

STEP 1. For the hummus, preheat oven to 375°F. Coarsely chop the bell pepper, discarding the seeds. In a medium bowl, toss together the bell pepper, garlic, 1 Tbsp olive oil, and ½ tsp salt. Spread evenly on a baking sheet and cook for 20-25 minutes or until soft. Set aside. Add tahini, cold water, lemon juice, 1 Tbsp olive oil, and ¼ tsp salt to a food processor. Process on low for 30 seconds or until smooth. Add the bell peppers and process for 1 minute or until well incorporated. Add the chickpeas and process for 4 minutes, stopping to scrape the sides of the processor bowl halfway through. If needed, add additional water or lemon juice to reach desired consistency. Transfer to a sealed container and refrigerate until ready to use.

STEP 2. For the tomato salad, slice tomatoes and onion into ¼" disks. Cut the disks in half. In a medium bowl, toss together all the tomato salad ingredients. Cover and refrigerate until ready to use.

STEP 3. For the cream cheese, chiffonade the basil (to do this, stack the basil leaves on top of each other, roll them into a tight tube, and slice the tube widthwise into thin strips). Transfer to a bowl with the cream cheese and stir until well incorporated. Cover and refrigerate until ready to use.

Continues on next page.

NOTE: The components can all be made several days ahead, but to prevent damp tortillas, the wraps should not be assembled more than 1 day in advance.

STEP 4. To assemble, spread 2 Tbsp cream cheese in an even layer on 1 tortilla. Spread 2 Tbsp hummus on top (alternatively, you can make some wraps with cream cheese and others with hummus). Layer on 1 turnip green torn into pieces. Spread 2-3 Tbsp quinoa on top. Slice the cucumber into ⅛" disks and layer 6-8 disks on top of the quinoa. Arrange ½ cup tomato salad on top. Wrap as you would a burrito. See grid below for reference.

STEP 5. Wrap tightly in plastic wrap and refrigerate. Repeat with remaining tortillas and fillings. Just before serving, cut vegetable wrap in half widthwise. The cut wraps can be served with the plastic still on to keep them intact.

Serve to Rabbit after a long day of gardening!

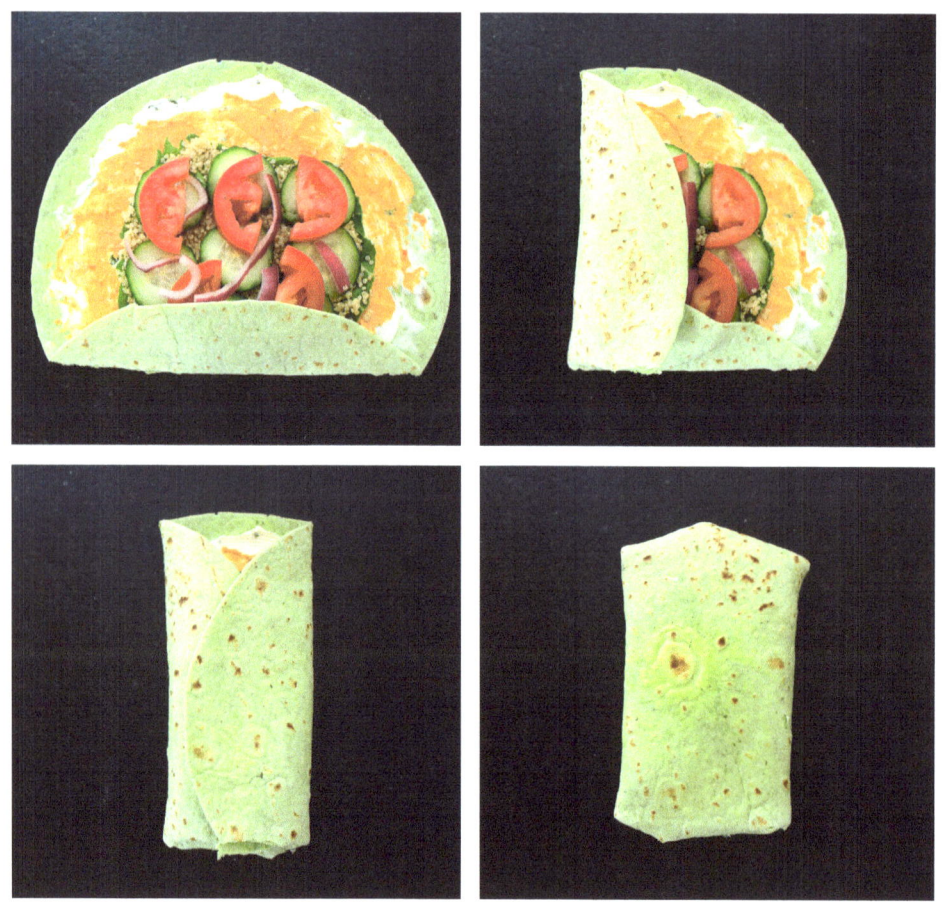

106

Tigger Stripe Fruit Leather

MAKES 14 FRUIT LEATHER STRIPS

"'. . . [Tigger] jumped at the end of the tablecloth, pulled it to the ground, wrapped himself up in it three times, rolled to the other end of the room, and, after a terrible struggle, got his head into the daylight again, and said cheerfully: 'Have I won?'"

Inspired by Tigger's orange and black stripes, these fruit leather strips are made with peaches and mixed berries.

STEP 1. Preheat oven to 175°F. Line a 9" x 13" baking sheet with parchment paper and set aside. Blend the peaches in a blender until smooth. Add the peaches, half the honey, and half the salt to a medium saucepan over medium-high heat. Stir to combine. Bring to a boil and reduce heat to medium-low. Simmer for 15 minutes, stirring regularly. Transfer to the baking sheet and spread with a spatula until even. Take care to make sure it's not thicker in the center, since that's the spot that will take the longest to set.

STEP 2. Bake for 5-6 hours or until tacky in the center, cracking the oven door a bit for 10 minutes every hour. Test the center at 5 hours by tapping it with a finger. When the center is set, remove the fruit leather from the oven and allow to cool on the pan to room temperature. Using kitchen sheers, trim the edges from the parchment paper and cut the fruit leather (still on the paper) widthwise into 7 strips. Roll the strips into tubes and secure with kitchen twine. Store in a loosely covered container at room temp. It will keep for at least 3 months, but starts to toughen after 1 month.

STEP 2. Repeat Steps 1 and 2 with the remaining ingredients, pressing berries through a wire mesh strainer to remove seeds before adding to the saucepan.

Serve while bouncing through the Hundred Acre Wood with Tigger!

INGREDIENTS

- **4 cups frozen peaches, thawed**
- **4 cups frozen mixed berries, thawed**
- **6 Tbsp honey, divided**
- **¼ tsp salt, divided**

NOTE: If the edges of the fruit leather are too crunchy to roll, you can cut them away with kitchen sheers.

 # Honey Clementine Cupcakes

MAKES 12 CUPCAKES

"'I generally have a small something about now . . .' and [Pooh] looked wistfully at the cupboard in the corner of Owl's parlour; 'just a mouthful of condensed milk or whatnot, with perhaps a lick of honey.'"

In honor of Pooh Bear's love of honey, these cupcakes are made with honey almond sponge cake, clementine frosting piped in the shape of a beehive, and handmade marzipan bees.

INGREDIENTS

For the Cupcakes
- 1 cup flour
- ½ tsp baking soda
- ¼ tsp salt
- ¼ cup butter, softened
- ½ cup sugar
- 1 tsp almond extract
- ¼ cup honey
- 2 eggs, room temp
- 2½ Tbsp sour cream
- ¾ tsp distilled white vinegar
- ½ cup buttermilk

For the Frosting
- 30 drops (⅜ tsp) orange gel food coloring
- 1 Tbsp milk
- ¾ cup butter, softened
- 3 cups sifted powdered sugar, divided
- 1 tsp clementine zest
- 1½ Tbsp clementine juice

For the Decorations
- 1 cup powdered sugar
- 1 cup almond flour
- 1 Tbsp orange blossom water or plain water
- 1 Tbsp simple syrup
- 1 tsp almond extract
- 3 drops yellow gel food coloring
- Brown food marker
- 24 almond slices
- 12 honeycomb-shaped cereal pieces

STEP 1. For the cupcakes, preheat oven to 350°F. Line a cupcake tin with liners and set aside. In a medium bowl, whisk together the flour, baking soda, and salt. Set aside. In a large bowl, beat the butter with a hand mixer on medium-low speed for 30 seconds. Beat in the sugar and almond extract until smooth. Beat in the honey. Beat in the eggs one at a time until just combined. Stop to scrape the sides and bottom of the bowl if needed. Beat in sour cream, then the white vinegar. Beat in half the flour mix, then half the buttermilk. Repeat with remaining flour mix and buttermilk. Evenly divide the batter between the cupcake liners and bake for 20 minutes or until cupcakes are golden on top and spring back when lightly tapped with a finger. Allow to rest in the pan for 2 minutes. Transfer to a wire rack to cool completely.

STEP 2. For the frosting, whisk the food coloring thoroughly into the milk with a fork and set aside. In the bowl of a stand mixer, beat the butter on medium speed until smooth. Beat in 1 cup powdered sugar until combined. Beat in the clementine zest and juice until combined, stopping to scrape the sides of the bowl if needed. Alternate beating in remaining powdered sugar and milk until fully combined, stopping to scrape if needed. Transfer frosting to a piping bag fitted with a large round tip (such as a Wilton #2A tip). Pipe frosting onto cupcakes in an ascending spiral to create the appearance of a beehive.

Continues on next page.

STEP 3. For the decorations, in a food processor, pulse the powdered sugar and almond flour until combined. In a small bowl, stir together the orange blossom water, simple syrup, almond extract, and food coloring. Add to the food processor and process for 1 minute or until a smooth ball forms. Knead the ball on a surface sprinkled with powdered sugar for 1 minute. Wrap in plastic wrap and refrigerate for 30 minutes. Shape into 12 ½-inch wide balls. Pinch the balls into ovals. Use the brown marker to draw eyes and 2 fuzzy stripes on each oval. Stick 2 almond slices between the stripes on each oval to create wings. Place the marzipan bees and cereal pieces on the frosted cupcakes.

Serve to a silly old bear!

Eeyore's "Feeling Blue" Iced Lattes

MAKES 3 CUPS

"'I have just seen Eeyore,' he began, 'and poor Eeyore is in a Very Sad Condition, because it's his birthday, and nobody has taken any notice of it, and he's very Gloomy.'"

You can make extra tea and freeze it into ice cubes to add to your latte before serving.

INGREDIENTS

- 4 cups hot water from a tea kettle
- ¼ cup dried whole butterfly pea flower blossoms
- 1 tsp dried chamomile flowers
- ¼ tsp vanilla
- ½ Tbsp honey
- Milk to taste (about 2 Tbsp per ¼ cup tea reduction)

STEP 1. Add hot water to a bowl. Add the butterfly pea flowers and chamomile and steep for 5 minutes. Straining out the flowers, transfer tea to a medium saucepan with the vanilla. Bring to a boil over medium-high heat. Reduce heat to medium-low and simmer 20-25 minutes or until the amount of liquid has reduced to 2 cups. Whisk in the honey until dissolved and transfer to a pitcher. Refrigerate until cold. Keep cold until ready to serve, then pour into glasses and add milk.

Serve when you're feeling blue . . . or any time!

Helpful Odds & Ends

Here you will find all manner of useful kitchen tips, charts, and lists. The menu cards, blank recipe cards, and testing logs can be copied or scanned for printing.

Printable Menus 115

Recipe Testing Log 124

Recipe Card 125

Cooking Tips 126

Conversion Chart 127

About the Author 128

Reference List 129

Index 130

Menu

The Queen of Hearts
Tarts

Card Suit
Tea Sandwiches

Mushroom Scones

We're All Mad Here:
A Dessert That Isn't as It Seems

Drink Me Potion

Menu

Delightful Applesauce

Curried Carrot and Chicken Sandwiches

French Carrot Salad

Marilla's Plum Puffs

Raspberry Cordial Italian Soda

Menu

Mini Bath Buns

Mini "Pigeon" Pies

Strawberry Fool in a Jar

Regency
Bride Cake

Citrus Mead
Punch

Menu

Orchard House Salad

....

Jo's Corned Beef
and Potato Roll Sandwiches

....

Pickled Limes
with Dried Fruit

....

Blanc Mange
with Strawberries

....

Plumfield Iced Tea

Menu

Peter Hat
Chips & Dip

Ham and Cheese
Pirate Ships

Neverland
Fruit Salad

Peter's Cake

Fairy Dust Punch

Menu

Blackberry Almond Croissant Bake

Carrot Apple Hand Pies

Chamomile Muffins

Vanilla Bean Marshmallow Bunnies

Strawberry Lavender Chamomile Iced Tea

Menu

Herbed Key Crackers

Fruit & Flower
Chicken Salad Croissants

Garden Gate Salad

Chocolate Raspberry
Cream Puffs

Sparkling Rose Lemonade

Menu

Honey Almond Granola Bars

Rabbit's Garden Wraps

Tigger Stripe Fruit Leather

Honey Clementine Cupcakes

Eeyore's "Feeling Blue" Iced Lattes

Recipe Testing Log

RECIPE	RATING
	☆☆☆☆☆
	☆☆☆☆☆
	☆☆☆☆☆
	☆☆☆☆☆
	☆☆☆☆☆
	☆☆☆☆☆
	☆☆☆☆☆
	☆☆☆☆☆
	☆☆☆☆☆
	☆☆☆☆☆
	☆☆☆☆☆

Recipe Card

RECIPE: _____

FROM THE KITCHEN OF: _____

SERVES: _____

PREP TIME: _____

COOK TIME: _____

TOTAL TIME: _____

NOTES

INGREDIENTS

METHOD

Cooking Tips

BUTTERMILK SUBSTITUTE. If you don't have buttermilk on hand for the cake or cupcakes, just mix 1 cup milk with 1 tablespoon lemon juice. Allow to rest for 5 minutes before using.

EASY DOUGH CUTTING. A pizza cutter is a great tool for cutting dough if you need straight lines or are cutting lots of strips (like for the Queen of Hearts Tarts or Rapunzel's Braided Pastries).

LIQUID VS GEL FOOD COLORING. I always use gel food coloring, which is more condensed than standard liquid coloring. This achieves a more intense color while introducing less water into the recipe. Gel is readily available in most grocery stores, but if you already have the right color on hand in liquid form, substituting is easy! Just add 2-3 drops of liquid coloring for every drop of gel.

ROOM TEMPERATURE EGGS AND BUTTER. We've all been there. A recipe calls for room temp eggs or butter, and we forget until it's time to start the recipe. No worries! Roll the butter flat between two sheets of wax paper and peel the paper away to reveal soft butter. For the eggs, just submerge them in a bowl of very warm water for 10 minutes before using.

SUBBING SALTED AND UNSALTED BUTTER. I ALWAYS seem to have the wrong butter on hand for a recipe. Luckily, you can swap one for the other with a bit of quick math. There's approximately ¼ teaspoon salt in every ½ cup of salted butter. Just adjust the salt content of your recipe accordingly, and you're good to go! Keep in mind that this sub doesn't work for recipes that have no salt at all, like some pie crusts.

STICKY MEASURING SPOONS. Having trouble accurately measuring sticky ingredients like honey because some of it always sticks to the spoon? Try coating the inside of your measuring spoon/cup with cooking spray. This can be done as long as fats like butter or eggs have already been added or will be added in the same step as the honey. Do not use this trick for recipes that cannot tolerate fat (such as meringue, which will deflate if even a tiny amount of fat is added).

Conversion Chart

OVEN TEMPERATURES

Gas Mark	°C	°F
1	140	275
2	150	300
3	160	325
4	180	350
5	190	375
6	200	400
7	220	425
8	230	450

WEIGHTS

Ounces	Grams
1	28
2	56
3	85
4	113
5	142
6	170
7	198
8	226
9	255
10	283
11	312
12	340
13	368
14	397
15	425
16/1 lb	453

VOLUMES

US fluid ounces	Milliliters
1	29
2	59
3	88
4	118
5	148
6	177
7	207
8	236
9	266
10	295
15	443
20	591
25	739
30	887
34	1 liter

About the Author

Alison Walsh firmly believes that food and books are best enjoyed together. In the 10 years she's been blogging at wonderlandrecipes.com, that belief has grown stronger every day.

In addition to blogging, she has traditionally published two cookbooks: *A Literary Tea Party* and *A Literary Holiday Cookbook*. Her first cookbook was a finalist in the cooking category of the 2018 Goodreads Choice Awards. Her recipes have also appeared on Mugglenet and the Good Morning America website. *A Literary Picnic* is her first foray into independent publishing, and she looks forward to sharing more such cookbooks in the future.

She lives in northern Illinois with her husband and two fae creatures who masquerade as children.

Reference List

Alcott, Louisa May. *Little Women*. New York: Penguin Classics, 2010.

Austen, Jane. *Emma*. New York: Puffin Books, 2024.

Austen, Jane. *Northanger Abbey*. New York: Harper Muse, 2023.

Austen, Jane. *Pride & Prejudice*. New York: Puffin Books, 2024.

Andersen, Hans Christian. *Fairy Tales*. New York: Barnes & Noble Books, 2007.

Barrie, J.M. *Peter Pan*. New York: Harper Muse, 2023.

Carroll, Lewis. *Alice's Adventures in Wonderland & Through the Looking-Glass*. New York: Sterling Publishing Company, 2012.

Grimm, Jacob and Wilhelm. *Selected Tales of the Brothers Grimm*. Ann Arbor, Michigan: Borders Classics, 2007.

Hodgson Burnett, Frances. *The Secret Garden*. New York: Barnes & Noble Books, 2005.

Milne, A. A., and Ernest H. Shepard. *The House at Pooh Corner*. New York: Puffin Books, 1992.

Milne, A. A., and Ernest H. Shepard. *Winnie-the-Pooh*. New York: Dutton Children's Books, 1988.

Montgomery, L. M. *Anne of Avonlea*. New York: Laurel-Leaf Books, 2017.

Montgomery, L. M. *Anne of Green Gables*. New York: Puffin Books, 2014.

Potter, Beatrix. *The Tale of Peter Rabbit*. New York: Penguin Young Readers Group, 2016.

Index

A
Alice in Wonderland 9-21, 115
Almonds 10, 12, 53, 59, 65, 83, 104, 110
Anne of Green Gables 23-31, 116
Austen, Jane 45-55, 118
Apple 25, 43, 59, 85, 95

B
Blackberries 12, 34, 59, 83
    Blackberry Almond Croissant Bake 83
Blanc Mange with Strawberries 65
Blueberries 38, 104
Butterfly pea flower 21, 113

C
Card Suit Tea Sandwiches 12
Carrot 27, 28, 48, 85
    Carrot Apple Hand Pies 85
Chamomile 87, 91, 95, 113
    Chamomile Muffins 87
Chocolate Raspberry Cream Puffs 97
Citrus Mead Punch 54
Cookies 17, 39
Curried Carrot & Chicken Sandwiches 27

D
Delightful Applesauce 25
Drink Me Potion 21
Drinks 21, 31, 43, 54, 67, 79, 91, 101, 113

E
Eeyore's "Feeling Blue" Iced Lattes 113
Enchanted Swan Cookies 39

F
Fairy Bread 34
Fairy Dust Punch 79
Fairy Tales 33-43, 117
French Carrot Salad 28
Fruit & Flower Chicken Salad Croissants 95

G
Garden Gate Salad 96
Grapes 38, 59, 74

H
Ham and Cheese Pirate Ships 73
Herbed Key Crackers 94
Honey Amond Granola Bars 104
Honey Clementine Cupcakes 110

J
Jo's Corned Beef & Potato Roll Sandwiches 60

L
Little Women 57-67, 119

M
Marilla's Plum Puffs 29
Mini Bath Buns 46
Mini Pigeon Pies 48
Mushroom Scones 14

N
Neverland Tropical Fruit Salad 74

O
Orchard House Salad 59

P
Peter Hat Chips & Dip 71
Peter's Cake 75
Peter Pan 69-79, 120
Peter Rabbit 81-91, 121
Pickled Limes with Dried Fruit 62
Plumfield Iced Tea 67
Poison Apple Punch 43
Printable Menus 115-123

Q
Queen of Hearts Tarts 10

R
Rabbit's Garden Wraps 105
Rapunzel's Braided Pastries 36
Raspberry Cordial Italian Soda 31
Red Riding Hood's Red Fruit Salad 38
Regency Bride Cake 53

S
Salad 28, 38, 59, 74, 95, 96
Secret Garden, The 93-101, 122
Sparkling Rose Lemonade 101
Strawberries 38, 51, 65, 91
    Strawberry Fool in a Jar 51
    Strawberry Lavender Chamomile Iced Tea 91

T
Tigger Stripe Fruit Leather 109

V
Vanilla Bean Marshmallow Bunnies 89

W
We're All Mad Here Dessert 17
Winnie-the-Pooh 103-113, 123

www.ingramcontent.com/pod-product-compliance
Lightning Source LLC
Chambersburg PA
CBHW041832060526
44119CB00105BA/338